Quality in Blended Learning

Concepts for a Quality Framework in Blended Learning

Peter Mazohl

Wiener Neustadt, 2015

Published by Peter Mazohl (Eigenverlag)

For additional copies, please contact
Peter Mazohl, H.O. Staglgasse 13, A-2700 Wiener Neustadt, Austria

Web: http://www.mazohl.at

ISBN: 978-3-901679-19-3

Editor: Peter Mazohl

Cover: Mag. Harald Makl MA

Graphics: Peter Mazohl

Language Support: Kathrin Zehrfuchs, Sophia Zolda

Manufactured by druck.at, Austria

druck.at
einfach | online | drucken

"[The] blended approach combines the best elements of online and face-to-face learning. It is likely to emerge as the predominant model of the future - and to become far more common than either one alone."

John Watson, North American Council for Online Learning (NACOL)

Content

List of Figures

List of tables

About this Book

Decades ago, teachers used blackboards in big classes full of pupils. The pupils listened the lectures of their teachers making notes by handwriting. Content driven teaching focusing on knowledge was the daily praxis. In the eighties, personal computers started to play a role in teaching, but did not change so much. The teaching methods remained the same. Technology was reduced to an overhead projector, handwritten slides and some videos based on super 8 films.

Today the teaching landscape has changed completely. Smaller groups of pupils follow the teaching using tablets or laptops; teachers have changed from content driven teaching to competency oriented teaching with a learner-centered access. Technology dominates the classroom; computers enable the access to the enormous knowledge hidden in the internet. Learning platforms are used to provide material, to carry group work, and to administrate teaching. This rapid development is technology driven and naturally in the new generation of digital natives.

In the last ten years the term of "Blended Learning" developed. This term describes a mixed teaching method combining face-to-face teaching with distance learning.

What is missing in all these new teaching methods is the development of quality assurance as a natural part of all teaching activities. There exist ISO/IEC standards, but they are kept very open and are process-oriented. Especially in Blended Learning, these quality assurance methods are not existing. This book presents a quality framework which is enhancing the existing standards and describes the problem field of quality in Blended Learning and provides a well-defined quality framework to develop the necessary quality criteria in teaching using that modern method.

1. Blended Learning

Teaching has changed in the last decades. The Austrian Ministry of Education started using Computers in school in 1985 (Fischer 1995, pp. 6). Since that, computers started to play a new and important role in teaching - not only in Austria. Computer assisted learning became popular. At the same time, eLearning started and developed - based on the Internet - to online (or distance) learning.

1.1. Significant Changes

David Wiley, Professor, Co-Founder and Chief Academic Officer of Lumen Learning, describes several significant changes in our everyday lives based on the development of technology and here largely brought to us by the internet technology (Wiley 2015). He mentions a change from analog to digital (that covers information, media, interactions, e-books), tethered to mobile (wireless internet, cell phones) as well as from isolated to connected (email, web services and other systems interconnect people) and from close to open (Open Source software, public available data).

People, who regularly use this technology, are permanently connected with the internet. They use their smartphone and their social networks, they are custom with multimedia and therefore they want to use all this technology in learning too.

1.2. The eLearning Hype

The eLearning hype of the last years brought some disillusion, as the method is not appropriate or sufficient for all problems (Bersin 2004, p. XV). Josh Bersin describes that in the early days of eLearning, dropout rates of 60% and more were usual. He located the reasons are the job situation and missing time, another problem is the missing social contact that is usual and typical for classroom lessons. Finally, the Internet-based content is often manifested as boring, slow, buggy and not fitting to the expectations. Courses were nothing else like pages of text with a few colourful images linked together on a buggy eLearning platform. Karin Asen (Asen 2013, p. 3) mentions in her interview with "Die Berater", an Austrian organization involved in adult education that the future of eLearning can be found in Blended Learning. The pure eLearning courses only provide knowledge, facts, regulations for product trainings and similar content.

1.3. Blend the Teaching

The solution of the described dilemma developed out of the positive experience of mixing classroom teaching with eLearning elements. Norm Friesen, Associate Professor in Educational Technology, Boise State University, mentions the first occurrences of the term in 1999 (Friesen 2012, p. 1). From that time, the development of the term started to the definition used in our days. Bonk and Graham published the first "Handbook of Blended Learning", followed with the book "Blended Learning in higher Education" from Garrison and Vaughan. Charles Graham defines Blended Learning as a system, "that combine face-to-face instruction with computer mediated instruction" (Bonk, Graham 2006, p. 5).

The use of Internet, the revolution of the Internet towards Web 2.0 and the high level of computerization of potential learners changed the definition of "computer mediated instruction" to distance learning using a computer.

That led to the distinguishing between online and classroom settings. Garrison and Vaughan define "Blended Learning is the thoughtful fusion of face-to-face and online learning experience" (Garrison, Vaughan 2008, p. 5). This definition comes near to the currently used praxis.

Asen (Asen 2013, p. 3) sees the future of Blended Learning connected with training content, which needs a contact person for the learners to answer questions. This will be a well-instructed professional trainer (or teacher), who cares for the learners in the phase of the classroom teaching, answering questions and explaining complex contexts.

1.4. Advantages of Blended Learning

Blended Learning becomes an increasingly popular method in teaching. Especially in the field of further education, Higher Education or continuous education in the frame of VET, you will find many courses or trainings based on Blended Learning. Here is a list of the main advantages of the method.

1.4.1. Saving Money

Classroom teaching - especially in further education - can be very cost-intensive. Travel costs and the subsistence for learners coming from abroad make the courses more expensive. Many subjects and topics can be taught in distance lessons; the classroom teaching is reduced to a minimum time to focus on necessary training. Here the teachers are able to use the additional class time to give it to struggling students. Battaglino (2012) describes in the report for the Fordham Institute several studies with a positive cost balance of Blended Learning.

1.4.2. Personalized Learning

Blended Learning as a whole offers the opportunity to personalize education in a way that is simply impossible in pure classroom teaching. Teachers standing in front of students are not able to take extra time satisfying the needs of each individual student. On one hand, Blended Learning allows students to work at their own pace, making sure they fully understand new concepts before moving on, while on the other hand, the teacher is available for extra questions.

Blended Learning includes a high potential for individualization in teaching. This aspect needs further investigation and research.

1.4.3. Individualisation

In the distance learning phase, teachers can concentrate on individual questions of students and streamline their instruction to help all students reach their full potential.

1.4.4. Flexibility in Learning

One of the most important advantages of Blended Learning is the flexibility in the distance learning phases. Blended Learning allows learners to do their lessons anytime and anywhere until a meeting with the lecturer becomes compulsory. On the other hand, the trainer (or teacher) is available during the classroom teaching to clarify all open questions, give additional information, support the learners with advices, explications, and be available for face-to-face communication.

1.5. Success Concepts for Blended Learning

Blended Learning concepts give the learners the opportunity to organize their learning effort, learning process and learning activities partly on their own. The precondition is that the employer supports these activities by additional measure. For this reason, an agreement by objectives should be obligatory and agreed between the learner and the employer.

Blended Learning is intensively connected with the maturity of the involved learners (Tabor 2007, p. 55) as well with the ability of self-paced learning. Learner expectations, especially their ideas that fewer face-to-face classes mean less work and the need to develop more responsibility for their learning and time management skills must be taken into account (Vaughan 2007, p. 84).

Learners have to understand the Blended Learning process. That requires a certain maturity of the learner. Consistent and transparent communication around the new expectations are helpful and must be a part of the preparation work.

1.6. Blended Learning Forms

In general, there exists a continuum of possible combinations of Blended Learning forms. Due to the typical and similar organizational forms of teaching institutions like schools, universities and adult education institutions four main models established in the last years.

1.6.1. Rotation Model

In this form of Blended Learning, students rotate between different stations on a fixed schedule - working either online or spending face-to-face time with the teacher.

In many cases, the detailed structure depends on the taught subject. Therefore, the Clayton Christensen Institute (Christensen Institute, 2012) defines a station rotation, a lab rotation, the flipped classroom and an individual rotation.

The rotational model is more widely used in elementary schools - 80 percent of elementary schools in California that use Blended Learning follow the rotational model - because many of them are already set up to have students rotate between stations (Christensen Institute, 2012).

1.6.2. The Flex Model

With this approach, material is primarily delivered online. Although teachers are in the room to provide on-site support as needed, learning is mainly self-guided, as students independently learn and practice new concepts in a digital environment.

The model is often used in schools with at-risk students or non-conformal learners.

1.6.3. The Self-Blending Model

The Self-Blending Model of Blended Learning gives students the opportunity to take classes beyond what is already offered at their school. The method is also well-established in adult education.

While these individuals will attend a traditional school environment, they also opt to supplement their learning through online courses offered remotely. In order for this method of Blended Learning to be successful, students must be highly self-motivated.

1.6.4. The enriched Virtual Model

In that method, students have required face-to-face learning sessions with their teacher of record and then they are free to complete their remaining coursework remote from the face-to-face teacher. Online learning is the backbone of students learning when the students are located remotely.

This model of Blended Learning is ideal for students who need more flexibility and independence in their daily schedules. It is a well-known principle in business and industry as well as in further education for teachers.

2. What are Blended Learning Courses?

Charles Graham mentions the term "Blended Learning" in the handbook of Blended Learning (Bonk 2006, p. 3) and defines it as a buzzword in corporate and higher education. It is one of the terms used besides distributed learning, eLearning, open and flexible learning or hybrid learning. More or less all these terms mean the same: Teaching is split into different parts taking place in different environments.

The traditional classroom teaching - following the thread above - is also Blended Learning: There is face-to-face education mixed with the distance learning from books in the homes of the students. From that point of view, Blended Learning is a very traditional and well-established teaching environment.

In our days, Blended Learning means basically the same - but the environmental conditions are completely different. Grown up in a Web 2.0 environment using technology means to communicate, to work and to learn, and those students are far distant from books. Students suck knowledge from the cloud, use the Internet intensively, and are determined by a world full of multimedia and interactivity. The young students are so-called digital natives grown up in a world full of electronics, technical equipment, smart phones and computers. The elder students and adult learners (most of them in a VET[1] program) are the so-called digital immigrants. The have learned to use the techniques, they are common with computers and the features of the smartphones as well.

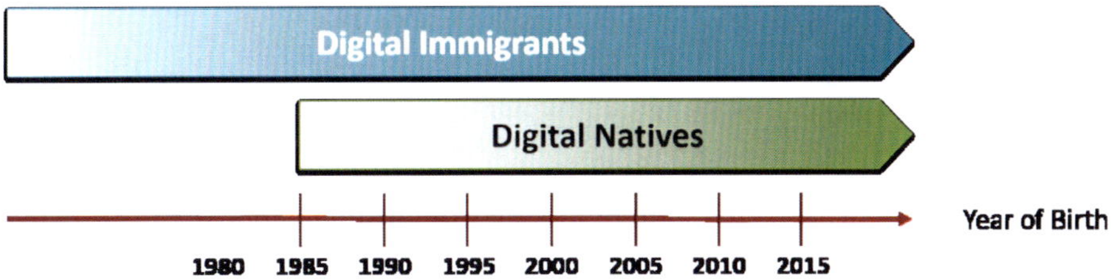

Figure 1: Digital immigrants and natives (based on Prensky 2001)

Therefore, it is necessary to give the term Blended Learning a new description. In this book, Blended Learning is understood as a teaching method split into

---

[1] Vocational Education and Training

face-to-face classroom teaching and technology based online learning (or distance-learning). This definition follows an idea expressed by Heinze and Proctor (2004). They define the only use of face-to-face teaching as classroom teaching, the exclusive use of online learning as distance education. In between, there are the different types of Blended Learning courses. The difference can be found in the dominating teaching method - sometimes it is the face-to-face teaching, in other cases the distance-learning.

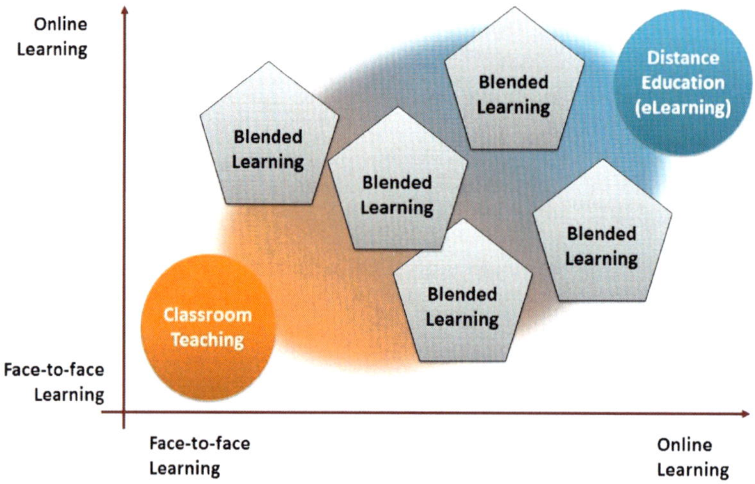

Figure 2: Concept of Blended Learning (based on Heinze and Proctor 2004)

2.1. Definitions and Frame Conditions

As mentioned above, there exist many different definitions of Blended Learning.

Charles Graham gave one of the first summaries of available definitions in the handbook of Blended Learning (Bonk 2006, p. 4). He describes Blended Learning as

- Combining instructional modalities
- Combining instructional methods
- Combining online and face-to-face instruction

The first two statements define Blended Learning so broadly that it describes almost virtually - more or less - all learning systems. Checking the existing learning systems, it is almost impossible to find a simple system, which is based on multiple instructional methods that do not fit to the description.

The third statement focuses on the method we are using in that book. Therefore, we will use the definition précised in the handbook (Bonk 2006, p. 5):

> *Blended Learning systems combine face-to-face instruction with computer-mediated instructions.*

In Germany, the well-respected Gabler Wirtschaftslexikon (Springer Gabler 2014) defines Blended Learning as:

> *"Unter Blended Learning versteht man die Kombination von unterschiedlichen Methoden und Medien, etwa aus Präsenzunterricht und E-Learning."*

Watson (2008) cites the definition of Blended Learning, used at the University of Calgary:

> *The integration of face-to-face and online learning to help enhance the classroom experience and extend learning through the innovative use of information and communications technology. Blended strategies enhance student engagement and learning through online activities to the course curriculum, and improve effectiveness and efficiencies by reducing lecture time.*

The Centre for Teaching Excellence of the University of Waterloo (2014) defines Blended Learning shortly:

> *"Blended courses integrate face-to-face and online learning. Online and classroom activities and course materials are selected to complement each other, to engage students and to achieve specified learning outcomes."*

Smythe (2011) finally offers a very up-to-date definition created by the Queensland University of Technology:

> *Blended Learning is a practical framework that can be used to encapsulate a range of effective approaches to learning and teaching. It encourages the use of contemporary technologies to enhance learning, and the development of flexible approaches to course design to enhance student engagement.*

The Clayton Christensen Institute, formerly known as the Innosight Institute, is a non-profit, nonpartisan think tank dedicated to improving the world through disruptive innovation. They define Blended Learning as:

"a formal education program in which a student learns at least in part through online delivery of content and instruction with some element of student control over time, place, path, and/or pace and at least in part at a supervised brick-and-mortar location away from home".

Heather C. Staker and Michael B. Horn (2012) give an overview of the current interpretation of the term Blended Learning.

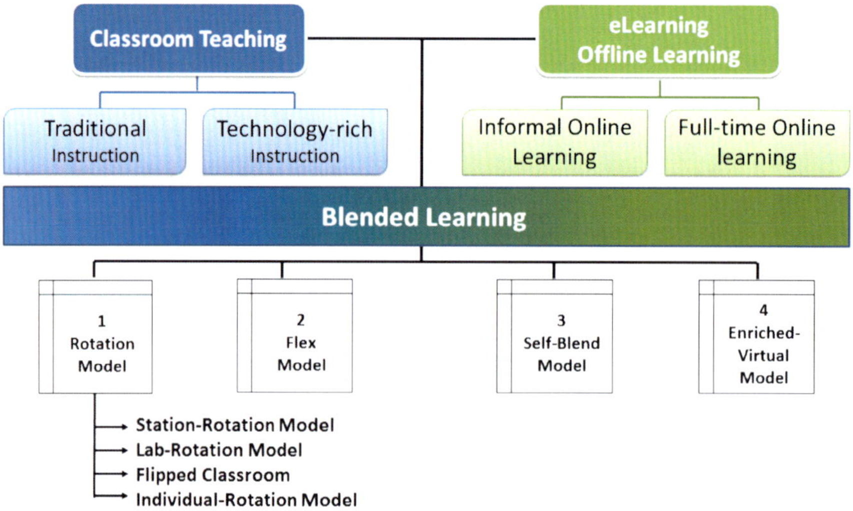

Figure 3: Overview of Blended Learning Models (following Clayton Christensen)

2.1.1. Dimensions of Blended Learning

The mentioned definitions demonstrate that there exists on one hand a similar access to the teaching method and on the other hand, there remain differences in the point of view. The description aim to the same instructional designed courses and finally they all include similar dimensions of the blend:

- **Self-paced and live learning**

  Blended Learning means self-responsibility and self-determination. The learner decides when which topic will be learned (including the "where" as well). Here we can interpret the "e" of eLearning as the leading letter from "every time" and "everywhere" and - maybe - "everything" as well (Anderson, 2008).

This issue is a crucial item of the distance-learning phase. Especially in further education, where the learners do their learning duty beside their job, this self-paced dimension is extremely important.

- **Offline and online learning**

  The well-defined splitting of the Blended Learning course offers optimized learning and training.

  The two methods are mixed.

- **Structured and unstructured learning**

  The face-to-face teaching phase represents a well-structured, well-planned and well-performed learning situation. Here strict timetables are used fitting to the limited available lessons in the classroom teaching.

  Contrariwise, the self-directed online learning is organized. Although the keeping of deadlines in the distance-learning is an obvious obligation for the learner it is his/her decision when (and where) the basic learning duty is fulfilled. Here the outcomes count (Guy 2013).

- **Lectures and labs**

  A lecture is probably the most standard form of teaching instruction. There exist different shades of lectures, starting from pure ex-cathedra teaching over variants that are technology supported ending at tutor-led working and discussion groups. The common ground of all these teaching activities is a teacher (trainer or tutor), who is available for questions during the complete lesson. This person can explain difficult context adapting the teaching pace to the directly given feedback of the learners.

  The comparable situation is in a lab. Labs are very similar to tutorials in which they also occur either before or after the lecture, and there are smaller groups of students working with a training assistant going over specific lab components affiliated with the course. Especial in labs, learning outcomes are covered which cannot been taught in distance learning.

- **Work and learning**

  Blended Learning is a suitable and appropriate teaching method for people being employed during the learning phase. Therefore, in many cases Blended Learning courses are so-called In-Service Trainings (IST-courses). They give people the possibility for additional or further training during parallel to their employment.

  Compared with eLearning, the face-to-face time offers more direct contact to other learners as well as the direct personal contact to the trainer.

2.1.2. The five Blended Learning Models

Bersin (2004) describes five well-defined and approved models for Blended Learning. All these models carry some strength and weakness inside. On the other hand, most of the training needs and necessary learning situations can be covered with one of the proposed models. It is good praxis to adapt a chosen model to the concrete needs and environmental conditions.

- **eLearning self-study with additional blended media or events**

  The central element of the course is the eLearning phase, a specific classroom teaching is not provided. The used teaching material can be offered online or on CD-ROMs or similar data medium. Besides that self-paced learning part, surrounding activities are provided, like online webinars with a tutor (or a team of trainers).

- **Instructor-led training[2] program blended with self-study eLearning**

  The learning program is mixture of instructor-led events and self-study eLearning. ELearning activities work as prerequisites, activities during the classroom teaching and activities between classes. The instructor led training as a classroom teaching in a "brick and mortar" environment should always be a good mixture of content, interactive students' contributions, different scenarios, maybe game-based or another specific approach to the defined learning outcomes.

---

[2] Instructor-led training (ILT) is facilitated by an instructor either online or in a classroom setting. Instructor-led training allows for learners and instructors or facilitators to interact and discuss the training material, either individually or in a group setting.

An example is the further training for teachers or other similar trainings in VET further education.

- **Live eLearning centered with other media added**

  The model is based on webinars, from the basis of the training. Additional, self-studies, exercises and references are provided as complementary activities. For this mode, we recommend the cookbook from Barclay (2003) for further reading.

- **On-the-job training centered**

  In that model, the on-the-job-training is crucial. That is typically done with a manager or an instructor. This model is often used for programs where skills are complex and must be proofed. The distance-learning part is usually done by traditional eLearning.

- **Simulation and lab-centered**

  This model focuses on simulations or the work in a lab. That model is often used where the learning situation gives the learner the possibility to learn and practice in a safe environment. That covers IT training, software application training as well as scenario based business skills training.

  An example is the training on network configuration, where you have the real hardware in the lab and a simulation program to practice the software configuration.

2.1.3. The four Christensen Clayton Models

Staker and Horn (2012) define a taxonomy of Blended Learning (in context with other education praxis). They define four Blended Learning Models:

a. The rotation model

Students rotate on a fixed schedule or based on teacher's discretion between learning modalities. Minimum one of these stations is managed by eLearning. Learning modalities can be organized in each proved teaching activities, for example, ex-cathedra teaching, group work in small units, group projects. The learning modalities never include homework assignments.

- **Station-Rotation Model**

  The Station-Rotation model allows students to visit various stations or centers during the allotted time during the course. This is done in a brick and mortar environment. Additional minimum one teaching modality is done online. The advantage of that system is the work in small groups at the single stations. So different needs of student's can be addressed more effectively.

- **Lab-Rotation Model**

  Sarria and Molina (2012) define the rotation-model implementation as a Blended Learning experience in which within a given course or subject students rotate on a fixed schedule or at the teacher's discretion among locations on the brick-and-mortar campus. At least one is a learning lab for predominantly online learning, while the additional classroom house is for other learning modalities. They are highly influenced by the publications of the Christensen Clayton Institute.

- **Flipped Classroom**

  A flipped classroom can be described as a model in which the typical lecture and homework elements of a course are reversed. That means that students learn at home using videos, documents or other materials and use the brick and mortar lessons for questioning the teachers, run presentations and do some group work. The preparation work at home is foreseen as a single work not connected in a community. Technology plays a big part in a successful flipped learning experience and students use mobile devices or laptops during their homework. Another critical aspect is the fact, that teachers need the knowledge, skills, technical equipment and the time to create or provide focused videos.

  The term is widely used and often focuses on prerecorded lectures followed by classroom exercises. In "Inside Higher Education" Pamela E. Barnett (2014) proposes a more peer integration in the home learning phase.

- **Individual-Rotation Model**

  The rotation is designed individual for each student (regardless if the learning modality is on- or offline). Using that method a better focus can be set on the individual needs of a student. That implicates that single-sided gifted students drop the parts where they have just gained the necessary competences but focus on their special training needs.

b. **The Flex Model**

The backbone of the student's learning is the distance-learning (may be realized in online learning as well as offline learning). Besides that, students follow an individualized schedule to attend or participate at miscellaneous learning modalities (brick and mortar). Different teachers provide a face-to-face support on a flexible and adaptive as-needed basis like small-group instruction, group work or similar learning activities.

c. **The Self-Blend Model (also called a la carte model)**

Students take one or more courses entirely online with an online teacher of record and at the same time continue to have brick-and-mortar educational experiences. Students may take the online courses on or off campus.

d. **Enriched-Virtual Model**

In the enriched virtual model, all students in the school divide time for every course between school and home. It differs from the flex model because students do not attend the physical school every day.

2.2. A Mix of Online and Face-to-Face Training

Blended Learning is a mix of traditional face-to-face teaching and online learning. The ratio does not matter (you can do 95% of your teaching in the classroom and add one online activity and it is still Blended Learning) as long as there exists a mix of the two. The question is if that makes sense.

A common system is to start with a face-to-face teaching, followed by distance-learning with the next face-to-face lesson. That can be repeated for several times. Finally, you have the assessment, normally done in the last face-to-face session.

For the classroom teaching it's possible to choose every proven teaching method or even a mix of techniques that fits to the expected competences. While the face-to-face phase focuses on practical issues (for example a lab) or on issues that should be explained from a teacher the focus of the online or distance-learning is set more on training, self-paced knowledge acquisition or other issues that can be learned easily without a teacher. Actually, the inclusion of the other learners in a peer group is also foreseen.

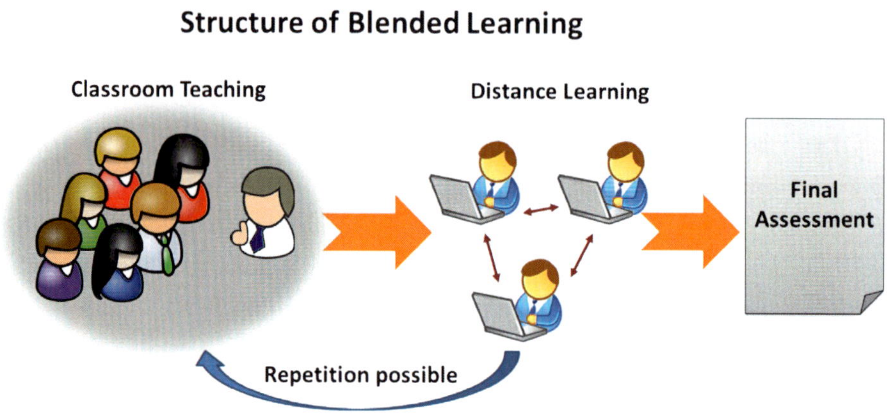

Figure 4: Structure of Blended Learning

2.3. The Physical School and the Virtual World

The face-to-face teaching is most successful, if the students' learning takes place in different locations, whether that's at school, in a lab, in a special location in context of the learning outcomes (for example in a museum if it fits to the topics), at home or somewhere in between. Obviously, most face-to-face teaching is done at school and most online learning done at home, but it is also possible to mix this up. For example, students can complete online work at a PC work station in the class or in the school library, and face-to-face teaching can be done outside the school building as well.

Learning is always a social experience. During the classroom teaching, there exist other students to talk with, they are available for communication and assistance and they all are connected to each other in a learning peer group.

In the distance-learning phase the learner is alone - maybe at home with the familiar contacts to friends and relatives, but missing the other learners of the class as well as the personal contact to class mates or teachers. That results in the creation of virtual communities. In the most cases the learners from the physical class meet again in the virtual world - maybe using a social network - but it is also possible to have people from outside in such a virtual learning environment.

2.4. Student Choice

It is typically for almost all learning environments that there exists a teacher or trainer that is responsible for teaching activities and modalities and still controls the learning process. In general that works the same in Blended Learning. Compared to traditional classroom teaching in Blended Learning there exists more freedom for the learner - combined with a higher level of responsibility.

A basic concept in Blended Learning is the intensive involvement of the learners, especially in the distance-learning phase. That includes some power for the learner to choose when and where to learn. This is an option towards personalised learning (Ableidinger 2013).

In the understanding of Blended Learning in that book, the distance learning is managed basing on eLearning principles. The “e” in this term can be seen as every time and everywhere - that is a special option offered by the online learning elements in a Blended Learning course.

The described quality framework for quality in Blended Learning is versatile for the different ages of the learners and covers the range from students in secondary education, VET education and continuous training as well as Higher Education (HE), and Adult Education (AE) and further training of adults.

A difference in that target group is based on the different learning methods and age-relevant behaviour in learning.

2.4.1. How do students learn today

Digital natives may own a high competence level in using ICT in everyday life. They are used to communicate with social media. Using emails is not so common in the communication behaviour and mostly relevant for sending information or material to the school/university or get information from there.

Most learning activities take place outside the classroom and social interaction is a growing part of learning. This is mainly done technology based: Smartphones, tablets or laptops (Chen 2013). Messages are sent using the messenger systems of social media as well as typical smartphone apps like WhatsApp, Telegram or other apps. This generation is more interested in IT and used to construct content than just to consume it - this is an advantage for the learning success in Blended Learning (Hoic-Bozic 2009).

Another feature is the intensive use of copy & paste from the Internet. To create this, content can be managed easily based on that technique, in the same way this practice decreases intensively the learning success.

2.4.2. VET learners

This group is often a mixed set of digital immigrants (especial in further education and training) and digital natives. The support level - especial for not so experienced technology users - is higher. Problems based on lack of knowledge in the frame of ICT occur mainly during the distance-learning phase of the course.

The social component is not so distinct and especial in VET further trainings you will find so-called "lone warriors".

In most cases, VET learners are highly motivated because the course is important for their job and they need to learn something new for their job. Many courses for VET learners are IST (In-Service Training) that are performed simultaneously to the everyday work.

2.4.3. Adult education

Here we will find a similar mixture as described in the chapter of VET learners. A difference is often found in the motivation.

2.4.4. Benefits of Blended Learning for students and learners

Besides the personal experience, the gained competence, the learning outcomes and the learning success there exist many other benefits for the students (Albrecht 2006).

- Blended Learning is the most flexible teacher based learning method
- The typical learning in a brick and mortar environment combined with an intensive technology based distance-learning builds technology and information literacy. This is a positive side effect additional to the acquired competences of the course subject.
- Blended Learning highly promotes active learning and increases the students self-control of learning
- The special situation in the classroom maintains special aspects of a classroom and leads to a good understanding of social cooperation during the distance-learning phases.
- Finally, the mixing of different teaching methods accommodates the different learning styles.

2.5. Face-to-Face Teaching

Teachers have had many years of experience in learning in face-to-face settings in classrooms, seminar rooms and labs. Although the face-to-face learning environments are often complex and unpredictable, teachers are very familiar with them and have developed high levels of skills in working in these environments.

The face-to-face teaching has been changed by the infusion of Information and Communication Technologies (ICT) into learning. That is evident in all sectors of education. ICT offers new opportunities but also new challenges for instructors and students.

Various teaching methods can be used in the face-to-face teaching in Blended Learning courses. In principle, two different access methods are possible: A teacher-centered approach and a student centered approach.

2.5.1. Teacher-Centered Approach to Learning

The teacher with a certain formal authority stands as an expert in the center of the teaching activity. Students passively receive the information and the content via lectures and direct instructions. This access is often connected with strict defined end goals and assessments.

The primary role of teachers and trainers is to pass knowledge in a most efficient way to the students. Competence oriented learning outcomes are a minor issue.

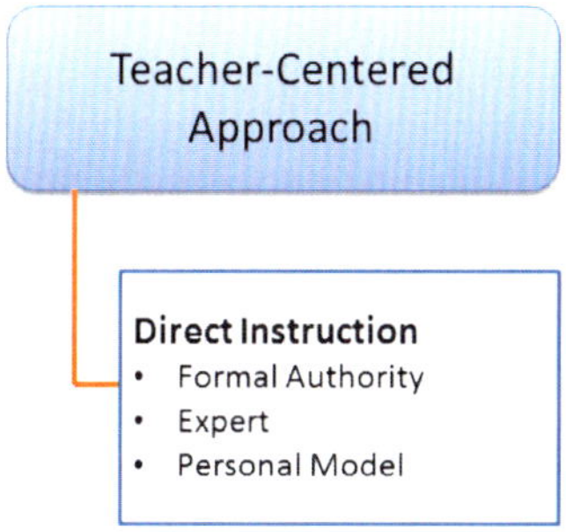

Figure 5: Teacher-centered approach to learning[3]

[3] See: Savannah State University: Pedagogical models

Grasha (1994) describes the three teachers' types:

- Formal authority teachers as being in a position of power and authority because of their exemplary knowledge and status over their students.
- Expert teachers are in possession of all knowledge and expertise within the classroom.
- Teachers presenting the personal model are those who lead by example, demonstrating how to access and comprehend information. The students learn through observing and copying the teachers' process.

2.5.2. Student-Centered Approach to Learning

Identifying feature for this access is the equally active role of students and teachers in the learning process. The teachers' primary role is to facilitate and coach the students, to set creative and intellectual impacts to the learning process. The students' learning is often validated through both informal and formal forms of assessments. That can cover group work, group projects, portfolio work as well as class participation.

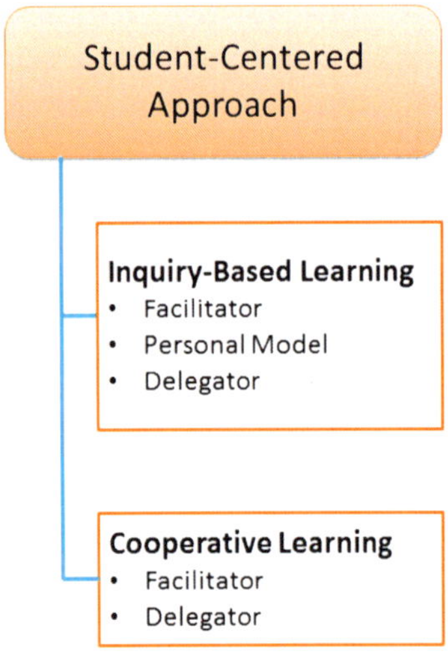

Figure 6: Student-centered approach to learning[4]

Froyd and Simpson (2008) give a well-described overview of the student-centered approach to learning.

---

[4] See: Savannah State University: Pedagogical models

Inquiry-based learning is a teaching method that focuses on student investigation and hands-on learning. The term facilitator describes a person that helps to bring about an outcome (as learning, productivity, or communication) by providing indirect or unobtrusive assistance, guidance, or supervision[5]. Students learn loosely guided by their teacher operating under an open classroom model with competence oriented learning outcomes.

The teacher, acting as a delegator, is a kind of resource for the students, answering questions to students and reviewing and supporting their work progress. Students are active and engaged in their learning. That is the first step for autonomous and self-determined learning and a basis for the distance-learning phase (Vaughan 2013).

Cooperative Learning refers to a common method of teaching and classroom management that is based on the social peer group of learners and emphasizes group work and a strong sense of community.

The teacher as a **facilitator** places a strong emphasis on the teacher-student relationship. Especially in an open learning environment, teachers and students are undergoing the learning process together.

The teacher acting as a **delegator** is concerned with developing students' capacity to work and learn autonomously. Students work independently on projects or act as part of autonomous teams. The teacher is available at the request of students as a kind of resource (Brannen 2014).

2.6. Distance-learning - or eLearning?

Sehra, Maghu and Bhardawaj (2014, p. 824) define the difference between distance-learning and eLearning:

> *Distance-learning is a sequential and step by step delivery system that connects learners, regardless of their location, with educational resources provided to them. The resources and a step-by-step guide are provided to the learner for keeping in touch with normal regular attending students.*
>
> *E-Learning is a term that refers to a wide range of electronically distributed teaching and training materials. It most commonly refers to*

[5] Source: http://www.merriam-webster.com/dictionary/facilitator

anytime, anywhere electronic or computer-supported learning and is often associated with online courses.

In the understanding of Blended Learning, the distance-learning is defined by the place where the learner manages the learning away from the brick and mortar environment. Therefore, distance-learning in this book (in the context of Blended Learning) has to be understood as a technology based kind of eLearning.

The most important fact in this part of Blended Learning is the self-determined learning method based on technology (Mazohl, 2014).

Distance-learning is well established and well researched in our understanding of Blended Learning. The distance-learning is realized in the Internet using a powerful and well-structured eLearning platform. The platform provides all necessary material, is used for group work and collaborative work and enables the communication between the participants on one hand and the participants and the trainers on the other hand.

Interactive and multimedia based content should be possible as well as the use of collaborating tools like wikis or forums.

In many cases, the platform is used for administration reasons as well. Many institutions - mainly universities - adapt freeware platforms for their special use and create an individual environment for students (see TUWEL, 2014).

2.7. Comparison of Distance and Face-to-Face Learning Environments

Learning has changed intensively and rapidly within the last decades. Technology in teaching gives students the freedom of permanent recherché, allows them to discover solutions to problems independently to teachers' lectures and finally is responsible for collaboration between students to reach better learning results.

Technology is as well the reason and the engine to split the learning process of the traditional school to interactive learning in two different environments - classroom teaching and the distance-learning phase.

Ni (2013) researched the learning effectiveness by comparing classroom and online teaching. Similar studies were done by Moriz (2008) at the Berufspädagogischen Akademie des Bundes in Graz (Austria).

Technology enables the design of learning situations that actively engage and guide learners while allowing them to choose the style of the learning experience and to organize the knowledge outcomes. On the other hand, technology cannot explain difficult context in that individual way as teachers do.

This need of coexistence was - besides many other facts - an impact to develop Blended Learning.

Comparing the two different teaching modalities, it is easy to find out, which part of a curriculum is to be taught in classroom teaching and which competences should be dedicated to the distance-learning.

In this brief summary, the most important pros and cons of these two teaching methods are listed.

- Online Learning allows the learner to learn at every place and every time. It is possible to access learning content easily driven by self-determination. In most cases, no special software is necessary to access information or data. The information transfer is easily facilitated by learning platforms. Collaboration can be realized easily and communication is possible without disturbing lessons.
  On the other hand, many learners need support either in technical issues for learning problems by trainers or teachers.
- Intensive group work or labs are typical for classroom teaching. Here the most intensive synchronous interaction is possible.
  On the other hand, classroom teaching may encourage passive learning with week teachers by only following the teachers' lectures.

The characteristics of the various teaching methods can be used to create a well-structured successful Blended Learning course.

2.8. Learning 2.0

The use of ICT in general and the social computing in particular have brought massive changes in various areas of society. The permanent use of the Internet with smartphones is evident as well as the fact that many people may be approachable by tablets or other mobile devices at all times. The shifting from verbal messages using a phone to write messages by messenger systems like Facebook or WhatsApp is a fact as well.

The use of ICT initiated massive changes in society, in the same way the learning conditions and teaching environments started to develop into a more and more technology based new teaching situation. New tools based on web applications were used in teaching. Wikis and blogs started to play a role in teaching and many organizations started to create web based learning courses including the new adapted tools and even social networks.

Many people call this situation built on technology based environment including social components Learning 2.0. Even if the term is popular in the Internet and Google offers approximately 31 Million search results on the keyword "Learning 2.0" the term itself is no standard and interpreted in a wide scope of meanings.

In that book, Learning 2.0 is defined as a learning environment giving powerful new options to collaborate, extend, enhance, and enable learning in an accelerated mode. Lance Dublin (2008, p. 1) describes the Learning 2.0 World:

In the

> *... Learning 2.0 world, which leverages the array of Web 2.0 tools, technologies, and approaches - including social software such as blogs, wikis, podcasts, videocasts, games, simulations, virtual worlds, and social networks - collaboration is an underlying principle, and the focus of learning is on the rapid creation, deployment, and evolution of a wide range of accelerated and powerful learning experiences.*

Actually, all the mentioned tools are part of a well-defined and equipped eLearning platform that can be used for Blended Learning.

3. Considerations about Quality The Five Quality Fields

Quality assurance frameworks allow defining an access to quality. These frameworks can be used as a versatile description of general quality issues. In education for specific teaching modalities, the framework has to be adapted with a more detailed focus on the specific teaching environment. Therefore, the framework is kept open and fits to all-purpose education situations.

It is important to acknowledge that quality of a learning process is not something that is delivered to a learner by a course provider but rather constitutes a process of co-production between the learner and the learning-environment. The organizational aspects are mainly researched and the currently used norms (like ISO) cover the quality fields of the course environment. Organizations in their structure and processes also can be qualified by the ISO norms.

3.1. Various Frameworks and Standards

Here are some examples of existing guidelines and standards for quality assurance.

3.1.1. European Network for Quality Assurance in Higher Education

The European Network for Quality Assurance in Higher Education (ENQA) defines a well-fitting framework for quality assurance. The recommendations are divided into three parts, covering internal quality assurance of higher education institutions, external quality assurance of higher education and quality assurance of external quality assurance agencies (ENQA 2009, p. 7). The standards can easily be applied to teaching organizations in the adult education.

The first part describes the European standards and guidelines for internal quality assurance within higher education institutions. That covers the policy and procedures for quality assurance, the approval, monitoring and periodic review of programs and awards, the assessments for students, the quality assurance of teaching staff, the offered learning resources and student support, the information systems to collect, analyse and use relevant information and finally public information.

The second part defines the European standards for the external quality. Starting with the use of internal quality assurance procedures, the description continues with the development of external quality assurance processes followed by the criteria for decisions, the processes to fit for purposes, the reporting, different follow-up procedures, a periodic review and system-wide analyses.

Part three describes European standards for external quality assurance agencies.

3.1.2. ISO/IEC 19796-1

The process model of ISO/IEC 19796-1 lists seven parts called categories within the life cycle of information and communication technology systems for learning, education, and training (Pawlowsky 2007, p. 6).

The following points are mentioned:

- **Needs analysis**

  Identification and description of requirements, demands, and constraints of an educational project

- **Framework analysis:**

  Identification of the framework and the context of an educational process

- **Conception/design:**

  Conception and design of an educational process

- **Development/production:**

  Realization of concepts

- **Implementation:**

  Description of the implementation of technological components

- **Learning process:**

  Realization and use of the learning process

- **Evaluation/optimization:**

  Description of the evaluation methods, principles, and procedures

The ISO/IEC quality standard provides a consistent method to manage, assure and assess quality. So a well-defined approach is ensured for course providers. They have to adapt the framework respecting the descriptions to their characteristic environment.

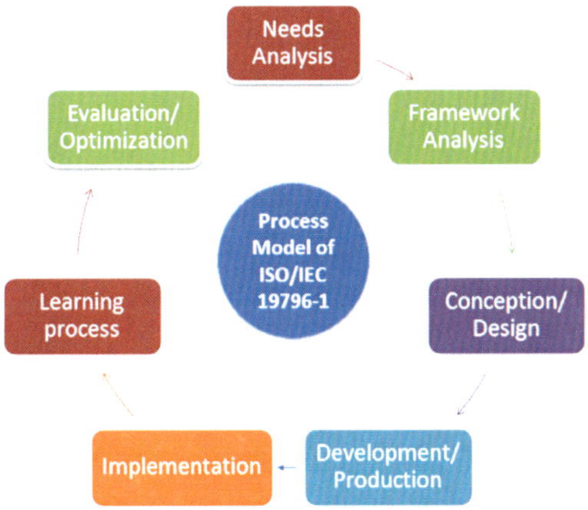

Figure 7: Process model of ISO/IEC 19796-1

3.1.3. Quality Matters, Inc (USA)

The institution **QM Quality Matters**, Inc. (QM) is a non-profit, international organization serving stakeholder in the online and Blended Learning industries. They have developed quality assurance processes and tools to improve and certify the design of online and blended courses. This means that the quality frame has become the national standard in the United States for course design. The developed standards of the company cover the complete scope of teaching in the States, starting from K-12 education over higher education right up to continuing and professional education.

The developed quality rubrics consist of eight general standards. These are split into various specific review standards. The system can be used to self-testing the course quality or for reviewers (educated by QM) to test courses. The basic rubrics are (QM webpage[6], 2014):

1. Course Overview and Introduction
2. Learning Objectives (Competencies)
3. Assessment and Measurement
4. Instructional Materials
5. Course Activities and Learner Interaction

---

[6] https://www.qualitymatters.org/

6. Course Technology
7. Learner Support
8. Accessibility and Usability

Obviously only courses are evaluated. The organization is not part of the review. The check of the rubrics' specific reviews standards show, that there is no specific competence model defined. The basis of the teaching is Blooms Taxonomy (Bloom 1972). Neither special quality criteria focusing on the learner are defined nor do there exist competence oriented learning outcomes.

3.1.4. Proposal to enhance the ISO standards with a focus on the learner

The process-oriented quality criteria are not the only success factors in efficient and successful learning. The Grundtvig Multilateral Project about "Quality in Blended Learning" identified five different classes of quality criteria based on the learner's needs. That means a new access to the learning and teaching process: the learner and the needs of the learner are identified as important factors. In this range, you can collect the different factors that represent the quality of teaching (Consortium Blended Learning Quality, 2015).

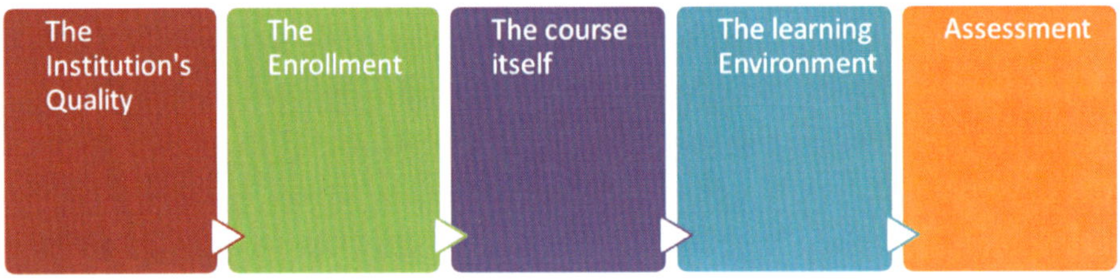

Figure 8: The five Quality Fields (from: QuiBL)

In the following part of the book, we will focus on items and quality criteria, which are in direct context with the learner, the learner's needs and the success of the learning process. In these chapters a description of typical Blended Learning settings, the situation of the learner and the context of quality is presented.

An entire description of a complete quality framework with hints for the use as a versatile concept for quality assurance is written in chapter 4.

3.2. The Quality of the Institution

The institution's quality can be described by a list of items in the quality framework by various European standards and recommendations. One option is to get the organization ISO-certified (for example in the frame of the ISO 9000 family), another is to run an analysis based on the ISO 9000 family to ensure the quality of the organization's processes and activities.

In this book, the institution is identified as any teaching organisation offering Blended Learning. That covers schools, high schools, colleges, universities as well as adult education organizations or teaching institutions focusing on VET[7].

In the Multilateral Grundtvig Project various quality criteria, which are important for the learners, were identified.

In general, a learner can expect offering a high quality Blended Learning course from an institution:

- The institution has a defined governance structure related to Blended Learning to enable clear, effective, and comprehensive decisions making.
- The organizational structure of the Blended Learning program supports the institution's mission, values, and strategic plan[8].
- The institution has a well-defined policy for intellectual property of course materials. That covers especially online course materials and public visible content.
- The institution has a high-level developed privacy policy for learners.
- The institution has a governance structure to enable systematic and continuous improvement related to the administration of Blended Learning education.

3.2.1. Administration

The administration of the course offering institution is the first access for the learner to the teaching organization. The administration is responsible for the interface of the learner to the course provider.

---

[7] Vocational Education and Training

[8] Defined by the Online Learning Consortium (former Sloan Consortium) in the Criteria for Excellence Quality Scorecard 2014

- **Technical Administration**

  The technical administration (normally based on ICT) of students as well as of courses must fit the current state of the art. The institution has policy and guidelines to ensure that the enrolling student is the same who is attending the course. Technology is kept state of the art.

- **Program Administration**

  The administration cares for consistency between the various sources of information provided for students, in particular between the examination regulations, handbooks, program specifications, and websites.

  The institution has a policy to cover all educational activities of the offered teaching and training programs with an appropriate quality assurance system.

3.2.2. Documentation

The institution has a process to ensure the necessary documentation for the teaching environment as well as for the administration of students.

A well-performed documentation is a key factor for good organization and it gives an impact to the learner as well.

Course documentation should be used for the course evaluation in the process of permanent amendments, especial for assessments, course content, course process, and staffing. Student handbooks for courses are a sign of care for good quality and help the students to manage the course.

3.2.3. Resources of the institution / Course provider

Learners have the right to expect a state-of-the-art equipment or resources in the teaching institution. These resources can be dedicated to three main fields:

- **Technical resources**

  The technology delivery systems are highly reliable and operable with measurable standards being utilized such as system downtime tracking or task benchmarking.

- **Human resources**

  The institution has a process for planning and allocating the human resources for planned and running courses. This means the classroom teaching as well as the tutorial support during distance learning phases.

- **Financial resources**

  The institution has a process for planning and allocating the financial resources for planned and running courses to ensure the learners progress and graduation.

3.2.4. Teachers/Trainers

Teachers and trainers build the backbone of the teaching process. They have to own a certain level of qualification in context with their teaching.

- **ICT Skills**

  Jan Gejel (2010, pp. 2-4) mentions the use of ICT as a general quality issue for Grundtvig Courses. Therefore, course teachers/trainers must be well-educated in the field of ICT. That covers on one hand the use of ICT to provide best quality of content, learning and interacting. On the other hand, the transfer of ICT knowledge to the learners is a permanent - but hidden - competence in all modern courses. This is valid for all Blended Learning courses.

- **Didactic Skills**

  Didactic skills are crucial for teaching. The teaching organization is responsible to supply the learners with best-educated teachers, who own the necessary didactic skills. Furthermore, the institution is responsible for the permanent continuing education of their teaching staff.

3.2.5. Instructional Design

There exist guidelines defining the requirements for course development, the course design and the delivery of materials (offline and online). That includes the course syllabus, various course materials, the assessment strategies and necessary feedback mechanism. Each course must define competence oriented learning outcomes.

The course design takes care that the embedded technology actively supports the achievement of the defined learning outcomes.

3.3. The Enrolment

The enrolment should be organized as an easy to handle transparent process. Additional to the collecting of data by the teaching institution it is also necessary to provide comprehensive information to the learner.

3.3.1. Students' information about the course

The institution has to provide sufficient information about the course. The learner must be able to decide if the offered course is satisfying the learner's needs. The summary of the course must include

- Simple facts like start and end of the course, exam or assessment dates
- A description of the competences that are taught (in the form of well-defined competence oriented learning outcomes)
- As not all learners are familiar how Blended Learning works, all-embracing descriptions of both the classroom teaching and the distance learning must be available.
- An estimation of the workload in general and specific for the distance learning phase. Optional hints for time management should be accessible for interested learners.
- A description of the used technology and the required technology for learners.
- Course costs (fixed and flexible costs)

3.3.2. Students preparation

Before the learners enrol into the course, they must be informed about necessary preparation work. That can be a simple list of pre-knowledge that is necessary to attend the course, a summary of the needed ICT knowledge or information about the necessary expertise to use the eLearning platform during the distance learning.

3.3.3. Student's group

Before the enrolment starts, the learners should get a clear perception of the course group. That is an important issue especially in inhomogeneous groups.

Learning groups can be inhomogeneous in many levels:

- Differences in ITC literacy
- Different learning pace
- Different ages
- A mixture of employed working learners and students without a fixed job
- Learners who are not experienced in Online Learning

Not all of this information is possible to provide to the learners, but the institution should care to plan and structure the learning environment to certain target groups and this information must be available before the enrolment.

3.4. The Course itself

The course as a Blended Learning teaching event is split into the classroom teaching and the distance learning. From the planning, there exists a certain schedule, which describes the rhythm of the switching of the two different learning phases.

Blended Learning courses have a target group of learners. This group is often identified by some more or less specific characteristics (Stacey 2008):

- They are interested in active and participatory learning and they are able to perform this in the classroom as well as online.
- They are common with the use of computers (laptop or tablet) and the use of the Internet.
- They are well organized and own the sense for a good time management.
- They are strong writers, creative but critical thinkers and experienced open minded communicators (necessary for peer learning in the distance phase).

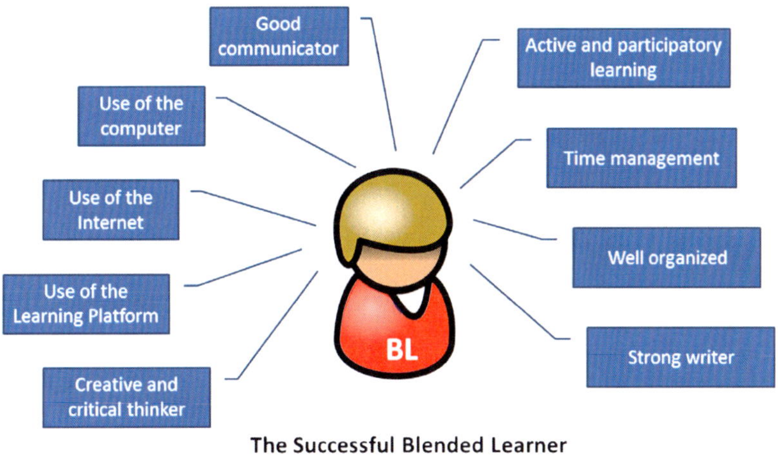

Figure 9: Skills and knowledge of a successful Blended Learner

A course of good quality is structured and planned to make concessions to the described students' features. The students are informed about the expectations set into them as course participant and should be able to self-evaluate if they are fit for their role in the course.

Students must be aware that the Blended Learning course is different from traditional teaching and that it is (in most cases) not possible to spare time in the learning process.

3.4.1. Course planning

Planning a Blended Learning course is not just transforming a portion of an existing course in an online environment. On the contrary, it is necessary to start from the beginning and to go step by step through the process of course development. Any common well-researched, tested and evaluated model for the instructional design process can be used to plan the course. For Blended Learning - focusing on quality issues to support the learner best - there exist some basic items to be considered in the planning:

- How do you allocate the teaching of the defined competence oriented learning outcomes to the classroom teaching and the online parts?
- Which of these learning outcomes are allocated to the distance learning?
- Blended Learning provides new opportunities for asynchronous discussions and working methods in groups. How will these issues be integrated in the distance learning?
- Is there a good schedule based on the allocation of the learning outcomes to split the teaching into class room- and online-teaching? Does this schedule consider the learners situation (especially the time factor and the problem of estimated work load)?

Important issues in planning the course are competence oriented learning outcomes.

In the European Community, the term competence typically characterizes a combination of knowledge, skills and attitudes.

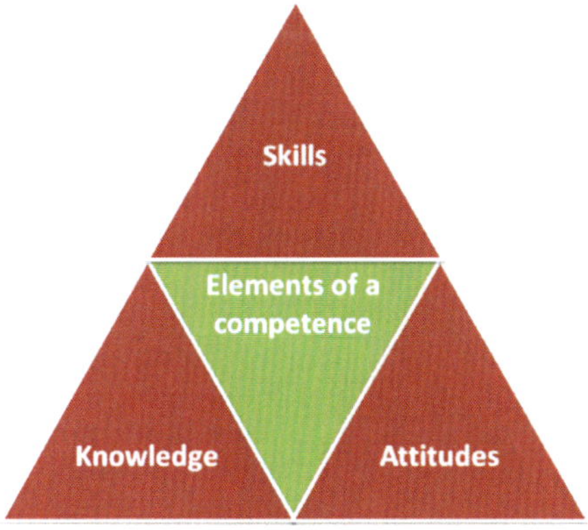

Figure 10: Elements of competences

The GINCO Network (2014) provides an easy access to develop competence oriented learning outcome.

Figure 11: Definition of competence oriented learning outcomes

The European Commission has defined eight key competences as an important aim to be developed in all educational environments. Therefore, in the European Community competence oriented learning outcomes are a kind of implicitness in European teaching.

Besides that, there exists the method of using Intended Learning Outcomes (ILOS). Sarah Mann (2004) defines aims and ILOS to describe the learning results of the course. She explains aims as "the broad intentions and orientation of the course or programme of study, i.e. what the teacher plans to do for the students and how", and the ILOS as "Intended learning outcomes (ILOs) carry a more specific meaning. They describe what the students should be able to do or demonstrate, in terms of particular knowledge, skills and attitudes, by the end of the course."

In general, there are small differences between the access of competence oriented learning outcomes and the ILOS. In any way, the teaching process focuses on the three columns knowledge, skills (activities) and attitudes.

3.4.2. Students activities

Blended Learning is more or less a kind of open learning environment. This kind of teaching forces the students to perform activities and to contribute to the learning. The activities might be forums, wikis, blogs, group work or other types of online or classroom doings.

Studies of Precel, Eshet-Alkalai, and Alberton (2009) show that the learning outcome depends partly on the chosen activity. They discovered that the students' attitudes differ in a broad range towards the pedagogical value of various instructional and learning components. (Precel, Eshet-Alkalai, and Alberton 2009, p. 7), in the scale from 1 (= no contribution) to 5 (= high contribution). The results present the printed textbook as the favorite and the personal notebook as the lowest awarded component.

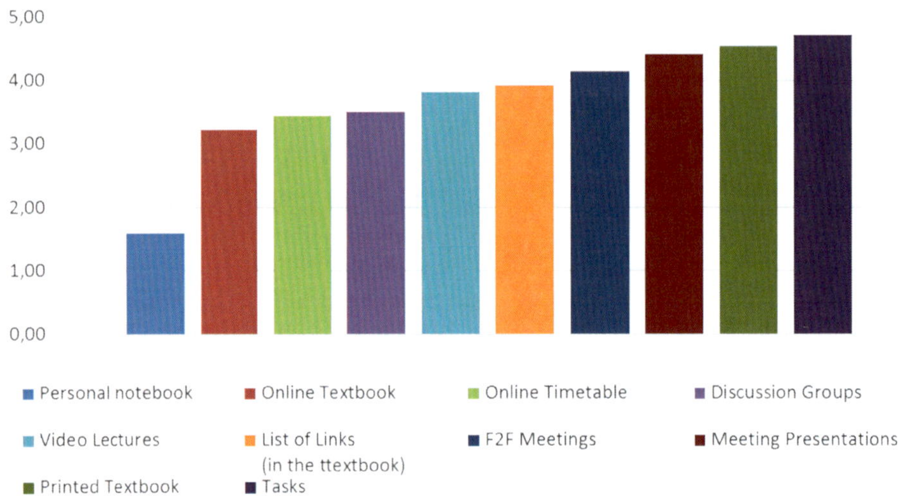

Figure 12: Preferences of students to learning components (Graphics: Peter Mazohl)

The personal notebook, a component in which students can mark selected sections from the online textbook, was the most unused component and was perceived as insignificant to learning.

This and other similar studies indicate that the use of tools and students' activities must be considered very carefully in the planning and design of the course to reach an optimized learning success. Planning a new course it is necessary to keep an eye on the students' activities and to provide subject-based doings for the students that fit best into the planned learning outcomes (both classroom and online teaching).

Kevin Yee (2012) describes around 200 possible activities in his essay that can be used in classroom and online teaching.

3.4.3. Students expectations

On one hand there are well defined learning aims (planned with competence oriented learning outcomes) when a course is planned and structured, on the other hand there are the students who want to attend the course and finish it successfully.

The course is planned for them and it is an issue of quality to care about their expectations.

- **The problem of minimum effort with maximum result**

  The basic expectations of students in learning are based on the fact that they want to be successful in learning with a minimum effort. This is a well-known principle from sports and business (Deva 2013) and it is not surprising that students behave similar.

  Therefore, it is necessary to ensure the learning quality to involve the students in the course in a way they accept it as a very convenient way of learning. Nevertheless, the teaching aims must be reached by the learners and the necessary competences as well as connected skills and knowledge must be available for them as a result of the course.

- **Understanding the concepts**

  Another issue is that students are often not so common with the concept of Blended Learning and do not understand the relationship between classroom and online teaching. They often expect less learning effort in the distance learning.

  To keep a high quality level makes it necessary to care especial for embracing information. Aycock, Garnham, and Kaleta (2002) describe in their document "Lessons Learned from the Hybrid Course Project" that from their experience "Students don't grasp the hybrid concept readily". They recommend paying attention to the students' expectation, their skills, their maturity or the time management.

  This part of students' support is a crucial quality issue and is a big impact to the learners' success in the course.

- **Active learning and time management**

  The problem of maturity can often be found with younger students (Prinsloo 2009, p. 53, 100). Most adult learners - especially in the frame of a VET training - have very precise perception and motivation for their learning.

  To ensure the learning quality it is necessary to support especially younger learners to understand their responsibility in active learning (Aycock, Garnham, Kaleta, 2002).

  The situation is likewise in field of time management, especially in the distance learning. The use of the internet, looking for online materials and the more or less permanent online situations distract students from their work.

3.4.4. Split the learning outcomes

The learners' success in Blended Learning courses depends on the kind of the split of learning outcomes. A well-planned and structured course cares for a well-defined allocation of the various activities. It does not make sense to split the learning outcomes and dedicate some of them to the classroom and others to the online teaching.

- **Criteria to split**

  All activities, which need the direct involvement of a teacher or trainer, should be done in the classroom teaching. That may cover explanation or illustration of technical issues or complex context. In the face-to-face situation, a teacher can react better to the students' questions and needs.

  Activities, which are based on peer work or cooperation, can be performed online in most cases. The practicing of content is also an issue for online learning. We have the same situation for reading or the summarizing and reflection of some content. The use of a learning platform offers the framework for joint development of knowledge or to create joint content from the learners' group. Supervision, guidance, and tutorial support can be done by teachers or trainers.

- **Activities dedicated to face-to-face learning**

  Here is a list of examples of possible activities during the classroom teaching. The quality criteria for their use is a meaningful use, well-done preparation, time economic handling and to comply with the defined learning outcomes.

- **Labs**

  They are a typical environment for practical work or hands-on technics. The practical work or the hands-on understanding with experiments fosters the skills and knowledge of students. Normally it is not possible to run labs in distance learning (there exist experiments with programming labs but there is no qualified study available).

- **Demonstrations**

  They are used to provide examples that enhance lectures, enhance the understanding and to offer effective hands-on, inquiry-based learning opportunities in classes or labs.

- **Film clips**

  They can be used in classroom teaching as well in online learning. In most cases the film clip is part of a typical classroom teaching activity.

- **Student presentations**

  They are an active part of peer teaching, improve the communication skills of the presenting student and the sense for critical adaption by the other students.

- **Group work**

  It contains to develop content in a group, find a context between different systems or questions or to develop some joint product that is presented by the group or discussed in a plenum.

- **Role playing**

  In many subjects it is an approved method to develop competences and to create content by the peer group.

- **Field trips**

  The personal experience of the participants in field trips can never be reached by online learning.

- **Editing and revision**

  Editing a paper and discuss the revision are typical face-to-face activities. Writing can be done as well in the distance learning.

- **Follow up on online discussions**

  After an online discussion (for example a forum session) in a face-to-face activity, the developed content is summarized, reflected and brought into fitting context.

- **Exams or assessments**

  Online exams are difficult to control, therefore in current praxis most of the exams and assessments are done in the brick and mortar environment.

- **Activities dedicated to Online Learning**

  Here is a list of examples of possible activities during the distance learning.

  - **Discussion**

    Online discussions use forums in the most cases. They can be moderated by a teacher or a peer.

  - **Reflections**

    These documents can be produced in the online teaching and published at the VLE. A teacher's review as well as a peer review are possible.

  - **Readings**

    The texts can be offered online or in print form. In any case, reading should be done alone during the online learning. Readings as a standalone activity cannot be considered as quality-oriented learner activities, they should be connected to additional doings.

  - **Remedial materials**

    This activity is used to supply learners. As there exist different learner types with various access to learning, there may occur cases where additional support for a special learner group is necessary. The best option to provide this material is online learning, where the self-paced learning has priority.

- **Group work**

  The VLE enables the group work by various methods. There can be a knowledge base developed by the group (a kind of glossary for example) as well as content can be created using a wiki of a FAQ-forum.

- **Self assessments**

  To test the gained knowledge, to proof the praxis in solving problems or to check the acquired competences a VLE can perform self-assessments.

- **Lower-stakes quizzes and tests**

  These are formative assessment techniques to monitor students' learning during the learning process.

- **Assignment submissions**

  The VLE enables the submission of general or specific assignments. Assignments can regard one learner or learner groups.

- **Lecture notes**

  In online teaching can be more time available to summarize the lecture notes and to bring them in a usable form. Lecture notes, as a reflection of the classroom lesson, can be an assignment for students as well (they can be published in a repository or an e-portfolio).

- **Lectures**

  Virtual lectures are very popular (2015). Big eLearning platforms like Coursera offer courses based on video lectures. In general, lectures based on a deeper understanding - often connected with some complex technical background - should be performed in classroom teaching. Basic knowledge, general information or less intellectual depth can be provided as online videos.

- **Podcasts**

  There are the visual learning types, others focus on voice and sound. The same rules as for the lectures are valid.

- **Case studies**

  This is a well-proofed activity to do the step from "knowing" to "doing". Case studies are a form of problem-based learning, where you present a situation that needs a resolution. A quality criteria is the mode of presentation of the results. The follow-up in a face-to-face session could be an appropriate solution.

- **e-Portfolios**

  The collection of learner-produced material on a presentation platform is an appropriate method to control and influence students' learning. The result as an e-portfolio can be a part of the final assessment as well. The work with e-portfolios is sometimes depending on the taught subject or the basic course structure.

  There do not exist many VLEs which support e-portfolios, in many cases VLEs provide basic repositories.

3.4.5. Technology

A Blended Learning course is always closely connected to technology. It plays a role in the preparation as well as in the classroom teaching (for example, the projection of multimedia bases presentations).

The distance learning is mainly affected by technology. That covers the use of internet, the possible interfaces (smart phone, tablet, notebook or PC) and the tools to fulfill the assignments or communicate with peers.

A quality criterion for the organisation is the use of the state of the art technology.

3.4.6. Engage students

For Blended Learning courses, the active participation of students is significant in all teaching forms. Therefore, it is necessary to engage the students as intensive as possible and to reduce attrition rates (Angelino 2007). The higher the involvement of students is, the higher the learning outcome will be. Consequently, the students' engagement is a quality criterion too.

There exist some basic approaches to engage students during the course. Methods are different in classroom and online teaching. To care for a high level of engagement the course provider can

- Develop rationales for the effective use of technologies to establish online activities

- Develop strategies for successful communication in the online learning (teacher - students as well students to students)
- Provide a good methodology mixture especial during the online learning
- Provide interactive assignments to keep the students active during the distance learning

3.4.7. Teachers' behaviours

Participants in Blended Learning courses are often learning beside their job, have commitments with their company or their families and are not available for learning all the time.

Teachers and trainers have to care for the information about their learners' situation and the possible workload - especial in the online learning. Good quality is proven if there is a well-balanced schedule between overloading the learners and running idle of the students.

This situation should be anticipated in the instructional design. Therefore, it is necessary to have a well-performed imagination of the future learners.

3.4.8. Duration of the course

The time frame of a Blended Learning course is always depending on

- The target group of learners
- The defined aims and learning outcomes
- The availability of the learners
- The possible work load
- The structure of the course (how many classroom teachings are necessary)
- Maybe on faculty policy (at universities such a course usually lasts one semester - sometimes two)

It is bad quality if the course must be restructured in time by rethinking about the course duration.

3.4.9. Definition of goals and learning outcomes

The definition of goals and the learning outcomes are an absolute critical issue in the development of a Blended Learning course. That can be reduced to the simple statement: No aims - no quality in the course.

The learning goals are the basis of the competences to be taught by the trainers and to be acquired by the learners.

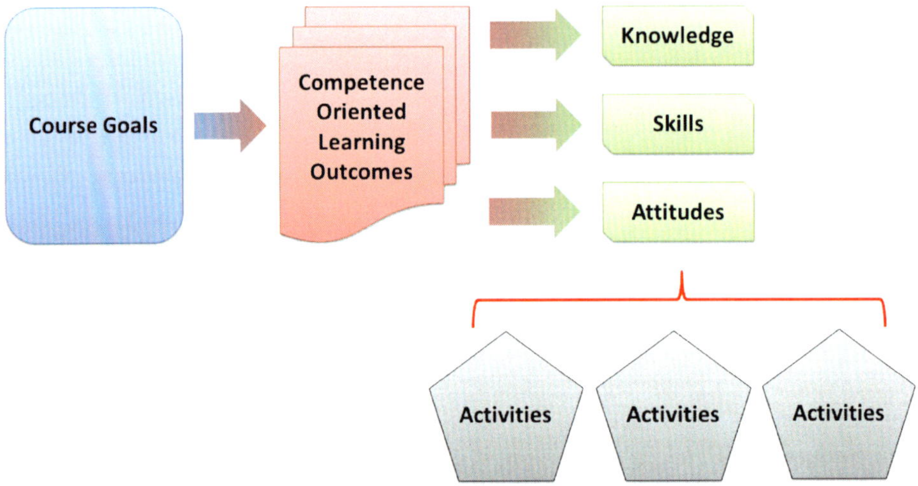

Figure 13: Definition of goals and learning outcomes

- **Course goals**

  These are broad statements of what the students will be able to do once they have finished the course. Goals are usually more abstract and use words like appreciates, shows, and demonstrates.

- **Competence oriented learning outcomes**

  A more concrete language is used in this outcome. This often includes the term "the student is able to ..."

- **Split of each competence**

  to the included knowledge, the expected skills and the attitudes.

- **The fitting activities are defined to each identified competence.**

  Depending on the type of the activity, each of them is dedicated to the classroom- or the online-teaching.

- **Evaluation indicators**

  For the evaluation of the competences, the necessary indicators are defined. Now it is possible to implement well-fitting assignments and to structure the necessary assessments.

- **Quantitative and qualitative goals**

  Finally the necessary qualitative and quantitative goals are defined to identify if the students have met the teaching expectations.

3.4.10. Learning approach

There exist various access methods as a learning approach. Different theories or approaches to learning complement each other and may even overlap. Blended Learning systems should be made up of elements of cognitivism, connectivism and constructivism. To support the learners best, the course provider should select an approach that fits to the taught subject as well as to the target group. In many cases, this is a mixed approach. There exist four possible approaches. All of them are well researched and proven. The preference in the European Community is on methods teaching competences.

- **Learner-centered learning**

  A learner-centered learning approach focuses on learning, rather than the content. Students experiences are an important fact, learning connects the content to real life. Students are engaged to construct the knowledge.

- **Assessment centered learning**

  This approach focuses on what students have to learn and what they need to know. Assessments occur before, during and after the learning.

- **Knowledge-centered learning**

  This approach encourages the students to think, to solve problems by providing various perspectives, to use and develop creativity during the learning and reflect what they have learned and developed.

- **Competence oriented learning outcomes**

  It focuses on the learning of competences. This causes a different access to learn the necessary knowledge, to develop and practice the various skills and to acquaint the defined attitudes. This type of learning is highly connected with self-determination and active involvement of learning.

To ensure the necessary teaching quality, each method needs a well-defined learner support as a quality criterion. They have to be developed as part of the teaching activities, mainly focusing on the online training. Teachers and trainers have to guide the learners and to conduct them during the course.

Hint: In this book, it is assumed that Blended Learning courses have a general competence oriented access to learning. Furthermore, learner-centered learning should be used as well. Therefore references to the learning approach are always aimed to access method including the mentioned issues.

3.4.11. Evaluation of course and student performance

The development of the evaluation of the course must be integrated in the course development. The evaluation has to be performed on several levels:

- **The course itself**

  This is the classic evaluation as described in the ISO norm and checks the teaching environment, the teaching itself and the satisfaction of the learners

- **Learning outcomes**

  In the planning and development of the course, learning outcomes must be defined parallel to the development of the course. That includes the necessary descriptions and indicators to test the new acquainted competences of the learners. With well-defined indicators, the learning outcomes are made measurable. To provide potential correction, measures evaluation should not be done only at the end of the course.

- **Teachers and Trainers including tutorial support**

  The quality of teaching is normally a subjective impression and reflects a personal opinion. The tutorial support is valuated similar. There are many evaluation tools that are adequate to evaluate that teaching field.

- **Course materials and technical equipment**

  The used training and learning materials as well as the available technical infrastructure of the course provider is another item of evaluation.

3.4.12. Teaching tasks

For effective learning, there exist several principles. It is the teacher's job to use them in a pleasant way to make it easy for the learner to achieve the learning aims and to do best in the course.

Quality criteria in the teaching tasks are an important base for the learner's success. Six major items can be listed: attention of the learner, perception and recall, organization and sequencing, instruction and feedback, learner participation and finally higher-order thinking (including concept formation).

Benjamin Bloom used 1984 some of these items. The new aspect is the use of technology in teaching and the changed learning and teaching environment. Therefore, it is necessary to see the mentioned quality criteria in the new context and to describe, how the quality criteria of the framework can practically be implemented in the Blended Learning course.

On the following pages there is an impact given about important facts in the implementation of the quality framework and what should be considered as teaching task.

- **Attention of the Learner**

  Attention of the learner in teaching must be implemented as bidirectional context between the learner and the teacher. To be effective the teaching must attract and keep the learner's attention. It is a kind of sender and receiver situation. The teacher must send signals and the learner must accept them.

  Besides the problem of the acceptance, it is a fact that attention tends to be individual, because the capacity to be attentive on one hand varies among different individuals on the other hand the same individual is differently attentive due to personal conditions and other influence.

  Nevertheless, to catch the learners attention is a quality feature and has to be considered in the course planning.

- **Perception and Recall**

  Mishra describes in the book "Educational Research" (2009) that perception requires that "the learner selectively focuses on and make sense of stimulation in the environment", including the learner's own internal states and responses (thoughts, feelings, and physiological states). Recall implicates the ability to remember, to reflect the prior learning and make use of it.

  It is in the responsibility of the teacher to provide events, ideas and concepts in a meaningful way so the learners can understand easily and remember to the content and the facts taught. A good method is comparison and confront learners with contrast situations.

- **Organization and Sequencing**

  These are well-known principles since 1984. The tasks of sequencing should be fixed in the instructional planning as quality criterion. A basic principle should be:

  The first and the last items in a sequence are especially important, as they are introductions and summaries and represent key learning opportunities.

- **Instruction and Feedback**

  Trainers and teachers must supply learners with skillful instructions and give a matching feedback (Hofmann 2014). That gives the learners the possibility to monitor their learning progress and work as well as an impact to the self-evaluation of the learners. Feedback is a tool for learners to discover errors or misconception and to recognize different strategies. Feedback should be done promptly and must fit to the learners' maturity. The feedback culture is a quality issue in the organization and a learner-centered quality criterion as well.

- **Learner participation**

  Learning implies engagement with the subject matter; this engagement entails some kind of performance. Activities that force the learner first to process something and after that to transfer the original information or learning content to a similar or new situation are working best to encourage the learner. To bring the learners to a high level of participation is a learner-centered quality criterion and should be incorporated in the instructional design of the course.

  Participation always depends on the will of the learner - they have the chance to choose a high level of participation for best learning results.

- **Higher-order Thinking and Concept Formation**

  The intention of concepts learning is often part of the process to engage the learner with other, related or similar concepts. That leads to problem solving by using previously learned principles and as a consequence to a higher-order thinking. All that supports the learning success especially in technical environments or in the field of physical lows or similar learning subjects. Higher-order thinking skills (HOTS) are a challenge in technology-based learning.

Teaching tasks are connected with the teachers, their teaching competence and experience. The teachers' quality is crucial for the learning success of the students and handled in part one describing the institution's quality.

3.4.13. Multimedia

Multimedia plays an increasing role in teaching and learning. Web 2.0 technologies have been widely applied for teaching and learning in recent years. It has been well documented that Web 2.0 Applications such as blogs, wikis, and online video sharing could enable students to collaboratively create content on the web. Web 2.0 applications, including web logs (blogs), wikis, Really Simple Syndication (RSS), podcasting, social networking sites, and peer-to-peer media sharing utilities are common to today's students, especial to the generation of the digital natives.

Mayer (2001) defines in his ongoing research seven principles how and why multimedia supports the learner (Summary from: Patrick J. Fahy, Media Characteristics and Online Learning Technology, 2008).

- **Multimedia principle**

  Students learn better from words and graphics or pictures than from words alone. The best learning results are acquainted by a combination of many media element (An obstacle is the limited capacity to process simultaneously presented media).

- **Spatial contiguity principle**

  Students learn better when corresponding words and pictures are presented near rather than far from each other on the page or screen.

- **Temporal contiguity principle**

  Students learn better when corresponding words and pictures are presented simultaneously rather than successively.

- **Coherence principle**

  Students learn better when extraneous words, pictures, and sounds are excluded rather than included.

- **Modality principle**

  Student's learning results are better from animation and audible narration than from animation and on-screen text.

- **Redundancy principle**

  People have only limited capacity to process visual and auditory material presented simultaneously; therefore, students learn better from animation and narration than from a combination of animation, generation, and onscreen text.

- **Individual differences principle:**

  Design effects are stronger for low-knowledge learners than for high-knowledge learners and for high-spatial-ability learners than for low-spatial-ability learners.

It is a student-centered quality criterion to supply students with multimedia content in their learning. On the other hand, it is a common error to believe, that every content must be presented in a multimedia way. Intuition, sure instinct is necessary to decide which parts of the course should be supplied by multimedia-based content and which part does not need multimedia supply. The feedback of students in the testing phase can be very useful as a basis for the selection.

- **Video**

  In the first ten years of this decade, the delivery of multimedia content especially in the online learning was difficult: low bandwidth, no standards and insufficient equipment of the learners. Today that is no topic. Interactive video platforms (like YouTube or Vimeo) allow the integration of content into VLEs or can be used as a video repository. The underlying technology is well proved and commonly used. Especial the modern tablets offer a wide scope of various programs or applets to use the available multimedia based content.

  The production of high quality videos has been simplified as well. On the other hand is the cost fact and - from the research point of view - it is not clear if there is always a learner's benefit for some teaching tasks.

- **Audio and sound (Podcasts)**

  The use of sound has similar parameters as the use of video. On the other hand, sound files can easily be delivered and are cheap in the production. Language learning has been identified as one of the disciplines likely to benefit from developments in podcasting (Rosell-Aguilar 2007).

- **Animations (and simulations)**

  Animations are extremely useful in teaching, especial in the online learning. In technical issues animations support the learner in the understanding of complex context.

  In the online teaching, animated simulations can be used to link together various facts and to increase the understanding, to answer questions that resume from the classroom teaching or to satisfy similar learning situations.

  Animations also have the problem of a high cost factor, especially if they provide complex simulations.

3.5. The Learning Environment

The learning environment contains two main items: the classroom teaching and the distance learning. It must be the main concern of the course provider to provide quality in both parts of a course.

3.5.1. The modern classroom

To provide a modern classroom and a well-equipped brick and mortar environment needs more than to provide some computers in the classroom. New concepts and new teaching methods far away from ex-cathedra teaching challenge schools, universities and teaching institutions. Smart classrooms offer a versatile furniture that can be used for simple teaching as well as an intelligent learning space for group work or other activities of the students.

Using the term classroom we address the facilities necessary for the face-to-face teaching - it does not mean a specific room but more or less the available infrastructure for the teaching process.

Hint: The book describes an all-purpose environment in a versatile quality framework. In various subjects there might exist the necessity of a specific furniture depending on the taught content. That must be planned and decided in the specific quality description of the institution.

A good infrastructure as a part of the quality criteria includes

- **A versatile equipped classroom for collaborative and ex-cathedra teaching**

  That includes a place where a stringent ex-cathedra teaching is possible. The technical equipment should provide a (modern) projector supplying all current available media.

  Additional for group work a fitting number of collaborative solutions must be available. Here problem solving orders, group projects or other activities can be managed by splitting the class into smaller units.

- **Sufficient electrical and electronically resources**

  Students often have their own equipment and have to plug their laptops to the AC. A wireless LAN (WiFi) should be available to connect to central kept resources as well as to the internet. A connection to a well-dimensioned printer is also an item.

- **High-tech lecterns**

  In rooms with intensive teacher- or trainer activity, a modern lectern must be available to control basic technical equipment. That covers the lights in the room, the connection to the projector, the control of the internet, the audio and video equipment and - if available - the interactive whiteboard control.

- **Flexible lightning control**

  In modern classrooms, it is necessary to control light more than the usual option of switching off and on. That concerns for example the function "room darkening" to create individual well-fitting light conditions during the presentation of videos or other image sources.

- **Flexible room size**

  Flexible room size can be realized by using divides in bigger rooms. In the most cases the room structure is given by the building, in that case several rooms of different sizes or partly separated areas should be foreseen to offer a well-defined splitting in work groups.

  The room problem is often managed by the administration of the school, university or the course provider. A well-defined and organized room plan and management for the course is a quality criterion.

Another item that must be provided in an optimized classroom environment is the general infrastructure. That covers a high speed access to the internet with a good bandwidth as well as the providing of configured computers for students without a laptop. Furthermore, for the electronically equipment a resource person must be available. This technical assistance has to clear doubts and queries in context with the technical resources. Additional the technicians have to care for the usability of the equipment and the error free status.

3.5.2. Communication and Collaboration

In modern teaching, collaboration of the learners is a request, a need and a fact. The traditional "chalk and talk" method of teaching may have still advantages (for example in basic mathematic lessons) but the cooperative modern teaching is more successful in most subjects. In very general terms, it is a fact, that the best learning success is acquainted by a well-planned, structured and performed mixture of different teaching methods optimized to the learning outcomes.

The goal of collaboration in learning is to give the learners the opportunity to communicate, to discuss, to collectively author, edit and review materials and to develop a community of the students. In that group of learners, it is an aim to work toward a shared outcome. Also in classroom teaching, there is the need of collaborative activities, such as peer reviews, sharing of experience of lab work.

The basic difference of the collaborative classroom learning to distance learning is in the fact, that a teacher or trainer is available and can support and supply the learners during their work (that implies that learning outcomes which must be intensively supplied by teachers should be managed in the face-to-face teaching).

Collaboration, at the conceptual level, involves:

- **Awareness**

  Students become part of a working entity with a shared purpose

- **Motivation**

  Students are interested to create a solution to a given order and so gain consensus in problem solving or development

- **Self-synchronization and self determination**

  Students decide as individuals how they get involved in the group learning process (is connected with the motivation).

- **Participation**

  Students participate in collaboration and they expect from the others to participate in the same way and intensity

- **Mediation**

  Students often share different points of view. Therefore, it is necessary to negotiate, to discuss, to collaborate and to find a middle point to create a well-adjusted group solution

- **Reciprocity**

  Students share and expect sharing in return through reciprocity

- **Reflection**

  Students think about given issues and consider alternatives

  Students are motivated to engage proactively

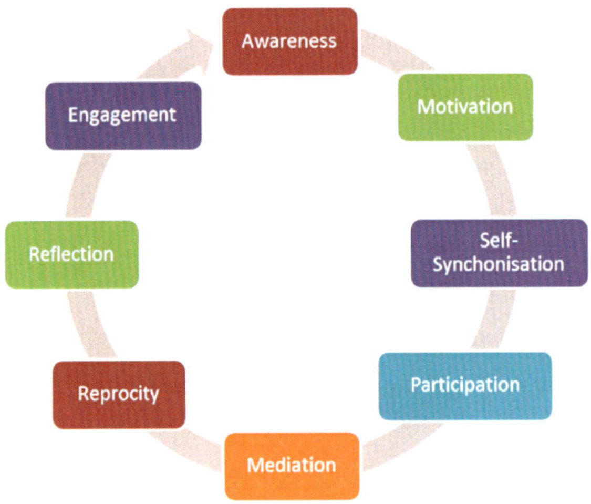

Figure 14: Communication fields

As a quality criterion - especially in the online learning - the course must contain well-defined communication descriptions. This information has to be shared with the students at the beginning of the course (and the students must be reminded on that issue from time to time). The teacher/trainer should monitor communication (as far as it is possible).

A basic quality criterion is the encouraging of communication and collaboration. That means either the communication between students and students as well as students and teachers. The collaboration is normally restricted to students or student's groups.

To perform a high level of communication and collaboration, there are several aspects to be foreseen in the basic course instructions. So all students should have the chance to express themselves (the monitoring is in the duty of the trainer or teacher). Students respect each other, disagreements are handled politely and everybody in the group contributes to the defined orders.

Another aspect of cooperation and collaboration is the preferred type: synchronous or asynchronous. Synchronous means an interaction of all involved parties at the same time. That is the standard situation in the classroom teaching.

Asynchronous defines a time-shifted interaction. The partners must not be available for the communication at the same time and that is the typical situation in the distance learning. Stein and Graham (2014, p. 26) mention that these two communication types are mixed in Blended Learning courses. They recommend not to replace a class room session by synchronous activities of communication.

3.5.3. LMS and VLE

In our understanding of Blended Learning we expect the use of a learning platform in the Distance or Online Learning. For learning platforms there exist several terms (or abbreviations) that are often mixed up, on the other hand there exists an overlapping description.

- **VLE (Virtual Learning Environments)**

  A Virtual Learning Environment is a software system designed to assist trainers or teachers to manage eLearning or Blended Learning courses. The system provides features like communication, assessments, document sharing and cooperation among the students. It provides elements of open learning with cooperation tools to build together learning resources.

- **CMS (Content Management System)**

  A Content Management System Is a software system to supply authors to create easily content in the Internet. It allows the creation and administration of online content by several people: pages are composed when requested by a user's browser. CMS offer multi-author features and can control the posting's history.

- **LMS (Learning Management System)**

  A Learning Management System supports the teaching organization with course administration an organization tools. It allows to deliver, to track and to manage a training. That enables to monitor the progress of the learners.

- **LCMS (Learning Content Management System)**

  This multi-user environment allows the course creator to develop, approve, publish, and manage online learning content. From the basic understanding, a LCMS offers tools inside the system for content creation.

The problem of the terms is the messing up of abbreviations. CMS can mean Content Management System as well as Course Management system.

There exists neither a recommendation for the best solution nor quality criteria focusing on the type of the used software. An overview of existing systems can be found at Capterra[9].

To create high quality Blended Learning courses there are several learning platform features necessary. Stein and Graham (2014, p. 22) give an overview of the common features of a LMS. The Blended Learning quality research team following ideas of Lorenzo and Ittelson (2005) and enhanced this overview.

Hint: The current policy in the EC is focused on the use of open source software. That is also an important issue for the eLearning platforms or platforms used in Blended Learning.

---

[9] http://www.capterra.com/learning-management-system-software/ (retrieved October 16, 2014)

The common features (as quality criteria of a Learning platform) should be:

Class Management	**Communication and Interaction**	**Organization and Resources**	**Practice and Assessment**
Class roster	Class announcements	Web page creation	Quizzes and tests
Grade book	Private messaging	Lesson sequencing	Surveys
Group management	Discussion forums	Outcome alignment	Online assessments
Peer review assignments	Live chat	File upload and repositories	Self-checks
Data tracking for learning analytics	Video conferencing	Conditional release	e-Portfolios
	Multimedia comments	Collaborative editing	Various rubrics (for example for grading)
	System notifications	RSS feed aggregation	
	Outgoing RSS feeds		

Table 1: Common features of a learning platform

It is a quality criterion that the LMS can easily be accessed by the students, offers a rigid navigation structure which is intuitive, easy to use with a stringent look and feel. A user guide must be available to know how to handle the various activities. The system must provide a clear and easy system to follow workflow. A training history must be available to collect trainings and assessments. Therefore, it must be advised against the use of a conglomerate of single web applications at different webpages as a LMS. In the late 1990s, web-enhanced teaching was a kind of do-it-yourself endeavour by giving the students a list of different addresses, which they had to use in the various online activities. Due to practical experience of the author it is obvious that these systems can not satisfy the students and trainers needs and should be refuses due to lack of learning success. That can be proved by the (non public) evaluation report of the pilot course about Quality in Blended Learning with Finnish teachers (Consortium Blended Learning Quality, 2015).

The expectations of the learners were summarized in a blog from Talluri (2013). He mentions similar issues as described above.

3.5.4. On-site Activities and Quality

This part focuses on the classroom teaching. The old role of teacher as lecturer and provider of knowledge has been replaced with a new role: teacher as facilitator, mentor and classroom manager.

During the teaching process, the teachers and trainers have to understand themselves as a facilitator, a mentor and a classroom manager. That requires the understanding the role of managers, leaders and facilitators and to live practically that role. Furthermore, teachers have to understand the students and have to meet or facilitate their needs and perform a continuous improvement. They have to be aware the quality criteria that are used in designing and building the teaching process. Teachers have to switch the teaching best fitting to the competence oriented learning outcomes.

The students have to be the active participants in the classroom. They have to be motivated, work for themselves as well as in groups - often in open learning environments.

Here are the most common classroom activities with a in a short description including some hints to quality criteria.

Activity	Description
"Ex-cathedra teaching" lessons	May used only in specific situations (For example, if it is the quickest and most economical way to reach the learning goals). The University of Technology Vienna (Akmath 2014) offers these lessons in their refreshment courses (based on Blended Learning) to bring the students as quickly as possible to the same knowledge level of mathematics.
(group) discussion on specific issues	Discussions can produce unmatched learning experiences as students express their ideas, respond or contradict to classmates' points, and develop skills

Activity	Description
	in evaluating the evidence of their own and others' position.
Presentation with peer feedback	Presentation of a solution or some work outcomes as a group and receive a peer feedback.
Problem-based learning	This activity consists of guiding questions; they often focus on quantitative problems.
Problem solving	That means collaborate mind mapping, the development or group grids or sequence chains to produce a visual outcome as the solution of a problem are typical group activities for problem solving.
Interactive Demonstrations	They are enrichments for lectures and can be organized with students help. Therefore, the learners are actively involved.
Lab work	That is the classical situation of on-site learning. The practical work can be done alone or in groups. Normally labs are personally monitored and supplied by trainers or teachers.
Role playing	For various subjects role playing offers a very intensive method to deepen new acquainted knowledge and skills.

Table 2: On-site activities

This partial list of examples demonstrates that there exist a big scope of different on-site learning activities. However, they have the need of an intensive engagement of a teacher, trainer or moderation.

Especial the group activities require a high quality level of the teachers to engage the learners, to moderate activities, guide the discussions or give feedback to activities.

The quality criteria dealing with the on-site teaching are the trainers' quality, the quality of the prepared material and the quality in guidance.

Distance Learning Activities and Quality

The difference between online learning activities to the classroom teaching are not so big - the difference is the environment. Students are normally at home and alone. Therefore, it is necessary to create activities that can be solved alone and with others, where the single learner is contributing to group work.

Here is an overview of various activities can be identified in online learning, with a brief description and some hints on necessary quality criteria.

Activity	Description
Case study	Case study involves an invented or a real situation. Students are provided with background information. Then, a problem is posed and questions are asked.
Investigation	This is an inquired-based learning environment where the following questions are asked: • What do we know now? • What do we need to know? • How do we find out?
Online debates and discussions	Selected and well-prepared topics with multiple perspectives are connected with questions and discussed in an online environment (maybe a forum, wiki or blog).
Virtual field trips	This is an option where you can explore a place you can't go because it's too big or small, too far, too dangerous, or just unrealistic. Virtual fieldtrips often include simulations.
Practice and testing	Students can practice provided examples (Körner, Winkler 2014) and different tests in an interactive web environment (Maple T.A. for example for mathematics).
Simulation	Here the work is focused on a real-word situation using a web simulation. Problems can be identified and solved without crashing the real-world environment.
WebQuest	This is an inquiry-based approach to designing effective web-based learning environments. The quests contain

Activity	Description
	an introduction, task, information resources, processes, learning advice, and evaluation. From the point of view of the author WebQuests are outdated and there exist better tools to replace them.
Tutorial & reading	These two activities provide new information. For enhancing interactivity, the teacher should consider the combination with discussions in groups or feedback in a forum

Table 3: Online activities

These examples demonstrate a lot of different options how you can define online activities. The quality criteria can be identified easily: Good preparation of the material (in close context to the defined competence oriented learning outcomes) with precise defined skills, knowledge and attitudes. Tutorial support as defined in the course description and monitoring of the activities is another quality criterion.

3.6. Assessment and Evaluation

Assessment is an integral part of teaching and learning. An effective and well-defined assessment can be used to engage students and can lead to enhance student outcomes.

Assessment can be understood from three different points of view: The assessment of the learning process of the learners, assessment as a learning process for students and finally the assessment of the course (as the part of a general feedback process for continual program improvement).

The Board of studies, teaching & educational standards (Bostes 2015, p. 1) promotes assessment for learning as an essential component of good teaching. In their advices of assessment (definition of standards), the three different accesses to assessment are described.

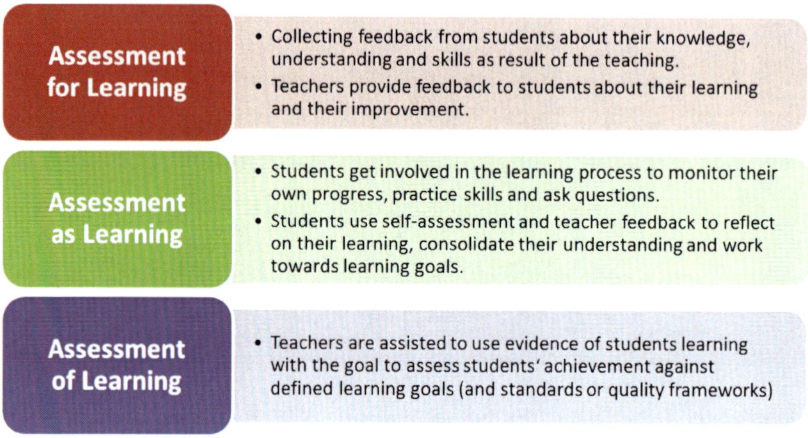

Figure 15: Different meanings of assessments

Assessment is a comprehensive name for collecting and evaluating of student's learning success. Assessment always has multiple purposes and should be a standard element in teaching. Interactive assessment methods can enhance the student's engagement in learning and can be a reason for motivation in the learning process (especially in interaction with teachers and other students).

The Board of Studies, Teaching & Educational Standards (Bostes 2015) refers to the below listed assessment goals:

- Provides opportunities for teachers to collect evidence of student achievement in relation to the predefined competence oriented learning outcomes.
- Enables students to demonstrate what they have learned, what they already know and can do now.
- Provides evidence that the current understanding is a well-suiting basis for future learning
- Clarifies the student's understanding of concepts and promotes deeper understanding.

As a conclusion of the assessment goals, the quality access to Blended Learning assessment must be valid and based on the defined competence oriented learning outcomes. In context with the course information, the criteria that are relevant and published for the assessment must be clear to the students. The assessment must be performed in a way so that the students can demonstrate their learning success in different context and proof the gained competences (that means free of bias and focusing on the knowledge, the skills and attitudes). Additional, the assessment should enable both teachers and students to get a feedback on the learning process. In general, assessments must be inclusive and accessible to all students.

Assessments should be used as a monitoring tool to control the ongoing learning progress during the course.

Assessments are also a teacher's tool to evaluate the course. It is a quality criterion that assessments are used to evaluate the course and be part of a quality circle for improvement.

The CIIA (2014)[10] defines assessment as an iterative feedback process for continual program improvement. They developed an Assessment Learning Cylcle (based on the classical quality management cycle, Commission 2004 p16).

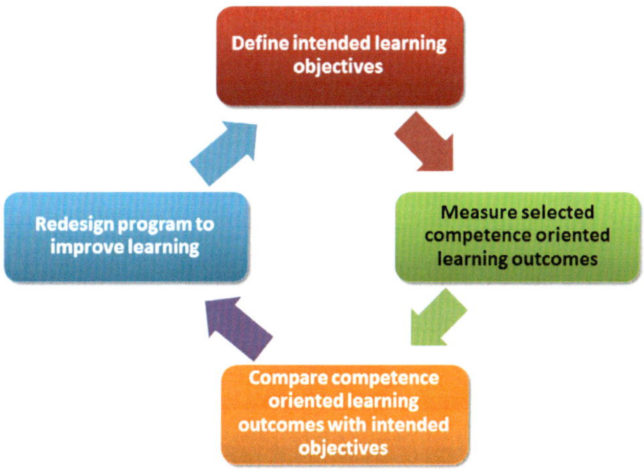

Figure 16: Learning Cycle[11]

The single steps are:

1. Definition of the intended learning objectives. It is a quality criterion to do this during the planning of the course or during the definition of the course structure. As well, the students are informed about the intended learning objectives.

---

[10] Center for Instructional Innovation & Assessment, Western Washington University

[11] See University of Oxford (2015): The Learning Needs Analyses Toolkit

2. The second step cares about the measurable competence oriented learning outcomes. For grading or evaluation of the learning outcomes appropriate measures have to be defined to get evidence how well each objective has been met.
3. Based on the collected data and feedback, it is necessary to compare the actual observed and checked competences with the intended course objectives.
4. Finally, the assessment results are used to amend the sections where the intended learning outcomes were not or only partly met. That leads to a redesign of the course. With these amendments, a new assessment circle starts with the next course.

CIIA (2014) defines the assessment circles as an integral part of student-centered education. The appropriate definition, performing and evaluating of evaluation are essential quality criteria for Blended Learning courses.

3.7. Conclusion

Ginns and Elvis (2007) tried to evaluate Blended Learning courses and to explore the relationship between online and face-to-face teaching and learning. Their study was defined as the beginning phase of development of a student-centered approach to quality improvement and evaluation of learning in a Blended Learning context. The also comment that there is a gap in the literature and qualified studies about learner-centered quality criteria that is (still) missing. The study's result can be interpreted that students vary in their perceptions of the Blended Learning environment, and that students' self-reports of their approaches to study and learning outcomes coincide with these variations.

The (small) case study of Dell, Low and Wilker (2010) demonstrates that the platform or medium (online vs. face-to face) is not as important as the instructional strategies employed, since there were few differences between in the quality of work from the online and face-to-face sections. That means that the Blended Learning method, based on well-defined quality criteria, can be a very successful method for the learners especial in the situation of employed learners in a VET further training program or other comparable teaching and learning situations.

4. Design of a Blended Course

Success in Blended Learning courses is highly connected with a very well planned and intensively supported approach, which includes a theory-based, qualified instructional model, a high quality faculty development, the necessary course development assistance, an appropriate learner support and a well-defined formative and summative assessment.

Success is also connected with the use of an appropriate quality framework. In this chapter, the new defined quality framework is used to describe the basic steps to create a high quality Blended Learning course.

The definitions of Blended Learning vary. There is no binding definition of Blended Learning. The (former) Sloan Consortium[12] (today Online Learning Consortium) defines Blended Learning as a course where 30% to 70% of the instruction is delivered online. This selection is taken from a table developed arbitrarily. While this can be used as a useful guideline, it may not be sufficient to define fully an institution's blended program. Furthermore, this definition depends on the learning aims (mainly in context with the subject), the learner's environment and many other factors.

Allen, Seaman and Garret (2007, p. 5) created the following table based on research results from 2004. They give an overview of the proposed proportional split of content and the description of the course type following the Sloan Consortium. However, in today's teaching, following the defined quality framework, the term content is outdated and should be replaced by "taught competences".

[12] http://onlinelearningconsortium.org/

Percentage of online delivered content	Course Type	Description
0%	Traditional (onsite teaching)	That is a course without any online technology
1 % - 29 %	Web Facilitated	A course, which uses web-based technology[13] to facilitate what is essential for a face-to-face course. Uses a course management system or web pages to supply the learners with content or assignments.
30 % - 79 %	Blended Course (also: Hybrid)	A course that blends online and face-to-face delivery. Substantial proportion of the content is delivered online, typically uses online discussions and typically has some face-to-face meetings.
80 % - 100 %	Online	A course where most or all content is delivered online. It typically has no face-to-face meetings.

Table 4: Classification of various courses

The description above originates from 2004. Ten years later, we developed a different point of view. The definition of the various levels is done completely differently. We will have a broader scope of different teaching methods, where Blended Learning is defined as a combination of onsite teaching and distance learning.

---

[13] Blended learning is not necessarily connected with web-based learning. The distance-learning phase can also be organized not-web based eLearning (like using CD-ROMS, DVDs or other non-web based material).

The University of Central Florida (2014) gives an overview of the different courses offered at the university. You will find a complete collection of different teaching types.

W - World Wide Web courses	They are conducted via web-based instruction and collaboration. Some courses may require minimal campus attendance or in-person/proctored examinations.
V - Video Streaming courses	They are delivered over the web via streaming digital video, which may be supplemented by additional Web activity, projects or exams.
RV - Video Streaming/ Reduced Seat Time courses	They provide classroom-based content over the web by streaming videos and therefore classroom attendance is not required. Other required activities that substitute for video instruction may include any of the following: web activity, in-person or proctored examinations and labs. See course notes for details.
M - Mixed Mode/Reduced Seat Time courses	They include both required classroom attendance and online instruction. Classes have substantial activity conducted over the web, which substitutes for some classroom meetings.
P - Face-to-face Instruction courses	They have required classroom attendance and meet on a regularly scheduled basis. Students may encounter internet and/or computer requirements in these classes.

Table 5: Types of courses at the University of Central California (UCF)

Very interesting is the use of **Reduced Seat Time courses** as a mentioned fact. Obviously, in this time economic learning (and teaching) is an issue of increasing importance.

The classical way to design a course must be driven by a careful planning of the course. An all-purpose plan should start with timing and logistics, the identification of the target group, the identification of the environmental parameters, the definition of the learning objectives, the development of an appropriate assessment strategy, the assignment of suitable instructional strategies, the design of the structure of the course and the schedule and finally the writing of a syllabus.

4.1. The five Key Elements

The use of a quality framework is the basis to provide high quality Blended Learning courses. Transferring the five quality fields discussed before you can identify five different items where the provided quality is directly connected to the learner and satisfies the learners needs.

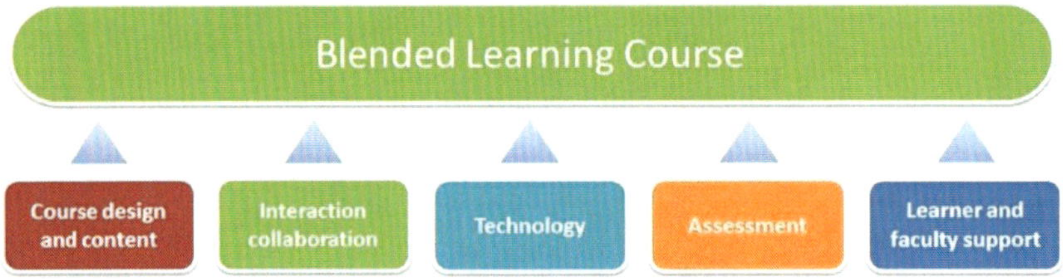

Figure 17: The five key elements in blended learning

4.1.1. Course design and content (subject)

The course itself is mostly based on content, which should be transferred to the learners. There exists the need to transfer knowledge in various environments (for example teaching at a university, special VET[14] courses, continuous training in companies or other reasons). A quality criterion is to develop the course to supply the learners best and to reach the best possible learning results. Content should always be part of the conveyed competence, included either in the knowledge part or in the skills.

To develop a course delivering some content, the following items should be considered:

- **Learner considerations**

  What does the learner expect from your course? Why did the learner select exactly this course?

  These and other similar questions have to be answered and are an

[14] Vocational Education and Training

impact to the course provider. In context of these answers, the institution or course provider has to provide an appropriate setting.

Due to these considerations, the knowledge about the target group is another important issue.

- **Learning task/content**

  In a well-defined modern course, content is a means to reach competences. The teaching should be organised by the definition of competence oriented learning outcomes (van Lakerveld, 2011, p. 5). They are the basis to define or create the learning tasks best fitting to the learners' environments. Now we have answered the question, which task is dedicated to the onsite teaching and which one is done in the distance-learning phase.

  The competence oriented access to teaching is an essential quality criterion for course development.

- **Instructional strategies**

  There exist various instructional strategies. In most cases, the use of ICT is included, especially in the distance-learning phase. Jan Gejel (2010, p. 4) promotes the intensive use of ICT in Grundtvig courses - but this is a general issue for all modern courses.

  The instructional strategy is the big plan to give an outline how the instructional activities will relay to the accomplishment of the learning objectives.

  A practicable way in Blended Learning is to care for sequences and clusters in the teaching process, to provide appropriate learning activities, to care for a well-fitting grouping of students (especially in the online teaching phase) and to plan a suitable selection of media in the onsite teaching as well as in the distance-learning.

  The intensive use of ICT is a quality criterion in course development.

- **Media and materials**

  Media must be a crucial component of active learning strategies and must be integrated in all learning processes (Niegemann 2007, p. 54). The well-balanced use of media is one of the secrets of success: Neither to overload the students with various media nor to avoid the input of media causes a successful teaching.

Materials must be prepared carefully and delivered in an easy and simple-to-use setting. The technical background of the institution and of the students as well must be well-known at that time to ensure that all students are able to receive all of the provided media.

The use of media is closely connected with the technical equipment of the institution as well as of the students.

It is a quality criterion to provide the students with the necessary information about the technical needs for their learning.

- **Learning environment**

  The learning environment must be well-structured and easy to handle with an intuitive user interface. Especially in the distance-learning phase there must exist a central point for each student to access the course or the course materials. In Blended Learning courses, the learning environment consists of the brick-and-mortar learning place and a designed information space (Dillenbourg 2000. P 3).

  To provide good quality, an appropriate onsite environment must be foreseen as well as an easy-to-use eLearning platform for the distance learning. The development of eLearning led to more useful learning environments as described by Dillenbourg, but the basic ideas remained since that.

- **Course design and preparation**

  A well-performed course design considers the topic and the level of the course. The students can be qualified into eight different levels of learners (fitting to the European Qualifications Framework[15] model).

4.1.2. Interaction/collaboration

Active onsite teaching is regarded as active interactions between learner and instructor as well as between learner and other learners. In distance learning environments, occasions for those interactions are often limited due to the system immanent setting. Modern communication technology has provided many tools to realise interactions and cooperation easily on a high level. In most cases, the base of these features is grounded on a learning platform or virtual learning environment (VLE).

---

[15] https://ec.europa.eu/ploteus/content/descriptors-page

Faust and Paulson (1998) propose small groups for effective collaborative learning - a group size that can easily be realised in Blended Learning either in onsite teaching or in the distance-learning phase. In that context, the precondition for success and for a high level of quality is an extremely carefully arranged course design and planning as well as the arrangement of complementary and well-structured groups of learners.

Pappalardo and Gunn (2013, p. 5) found out in their study that the "solving in groups" in classroom teaching was the best creating activity in learning. In addition, the explanations of other students were validated as useful in learning.

So and Brush (2008) mention in a small case study, that "Collaborative Learning experience in the computer-mediated communication environment is better than in a face-to-face learning environment" (40% of the students agreed to that statement). In the same study, they found out that Collaborative Learning in the group was time-consuming.

In an appropriate quality framework, these impacts must be considered as specific factors in context of students' satisfaction and students' needs. It seems to be necessary to create a well-balanced strategy between the use of active learning settings and the factor of time for economical learning.

4.1.3. Technology

Technology plays an important role in modern teaching. The US Department for Education published the vision that in education it is necessary to integrate current and future information and communication technology into everyday teaching and learning (Johnston and Barker 2002, p. 139).

During the development of the course, the following questions should be answered - the results must be used as an impact in the information of the students and - if necessary - in further trainings for the teachers:

- What types of technological tools are available to teachers and learners?
- Do these tools work appropriately for the pursued teaching and learning goals?
- Are all teachers and learners familiar with the used technology?

The questions mentioned above cause a list of used tools (in most cases software) and a description of the technical requirements to use these tools.

Horn (2012) mentions in his blog[16] that technology has not been ready for Blended Learning and proprietary systems yet - especially software - is only useful to get out data but - in many cases - does not offer the necessary modular architecture.

In an appropriate quality framework, the use of technology must be described very seriously (in many cases this description differs from course to course and must be created in the context of the course settings). These descriptions must include the various responsibilities as well:

- Who is responsible for the purchase of software?
- Which licenses or license models are available (for example, does there exist a campus license)?
- Is it possible for students to use the campus software during the course or purchase their own licenses?

The technology used in teaching processes must be seen as a means to reach a goal - technology is finally one of the tools used in teaching, especially in Blended Learning.

4.1.4. Assessment

Assessments are necessary in teaching - especially for the awarding of credit points or other strictly defined validation of learning. That causes the development of appropriate assessment strategies for a Blended Learning course.

Assessments in general are methods to get feedback from the students. That feedback - for example - may cover the student's performance, the increase of knowledge, use of skills or increase of competences.

Typical assessment methods can be classified in

- **Diagnostic assessment (sometimes an entry test)**

  Assesses the student's strengths, weaknesses, knowledge and skills (prior to the instructions).

- **Formative assessment**

  Assesses a student's performance during instructions, lectures and online activities. These types of assessment should occur regularly

[16] Blend My Learning, http://www.blendmylearning.com

during the teaching process. They can give clear information about the students' progress.

They are also an appropriate means for a fed forward into an instructional model that allows for responsiveness to students' needs.

- **Summative assessment**

  Measures a student's achievement at the end of the instruction.

  They supply teachers and students with the necessary information about attainment of knowledge. In modern teaching, the pure knowledge check is not sufficient and should be replaced by the check of competences (in reference to the defined competence oriented learning outcomes).

- **Norm-referenced assessment**

  Compares a student's performance with a national (or international) or other "norm" group.

- **Criterion-referenced assessment**

  Measures a student's performance with a goal, specific objectives or standards.

- **Interim-benchmark assessments**

  This is an evaluation of a student's performance at periodic intervals. Such assessments should be done at the end of a grading period. The results give information about the current performance and offer the option of some prediction of the summative assessment's result.

  To perform these assessments, three main delivery methods are available: paper and pencil, online or computer adaptive testing.

Assessments should be done as a blend (in onsite teaching and distance learning) in Blended Learning courses. The summary can be used for the grading of the students.

Assessments can be used for the facilitation of learning in different ways. Adjustments in various levels can be set due of the assessment results.

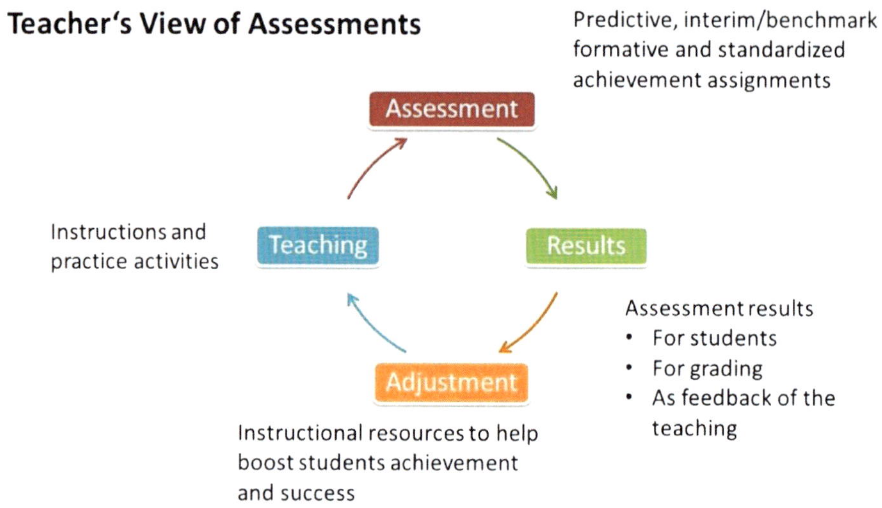

Figure 18: Assessments as versatile tool for teachers

4.1.5. Learner/faculty support

Teaching for an institution, school or university necessitates a certain faculty support as well as an appropriate students' support.

Faculty support concerns several - mainly organisational - issues. Here are some examples:

- **Technical Support** (hardware and software)

  Support for the teachers in technical issues (mainly focusing on ICT based teaching, software or browser problems, and others)

- **Instructional Support**
- **Personal assistance for labs or field studies**

Learner or students support has developed as a technical term for a particular set of practices, which have been developed within open and distance learning (Thorpe 2002, p. 106). Another common name is tutorial support, which means the support of students by their tutors.

Students do not only need various types of support during the learning process, they often want them and request for an appropriate support. The reason may be found in the condition that the environment - in situations of open and student-centered learning - is not defined very strictly, especially within Web-supported learning environments. Learner-centered learning environments may produce an unsureness about special learning issues and the students need some support to clear open questions. Depending from the learning environment, there are many segments and domains in which the teaching institution may support the learner.

In a well-defined quality framework, the description of learner support is necessary. The teaching institution must inform the learners about the supporting means offered to the learners. The scope reaches from the enrolment over the teaching phases until the assessment and the graduation. Each type of student support should use defined and appropriate methods, which should be well-defined and tested.

The success or failure of a student support system can be judged on a number of performance indicators:

- Developed under respect of didactic manners
- Provides an intuitive interface with a high level of usability to make sure that the human computer Interface is easy to understand
- Every person which has to, or wants to use the system, must have the technical requirements to do so
- Student support service is including the necessary technical support

Student support consists of a sum of arrangements to cover the needs of students. That can be:

- In the prospective or start-up phase of the course
  - Information about the course
  - Guidance for the various (learning) programs
  - Guidance on practical matters
  - Organisational issues
- Teaching (onsite and online)
  - Technical and software support
  - Personal contact to the tutors
  - Tutorials and guides for eLearning and distance education
  - Problems with assignments
  - Problems with assessments
- Graduation
  - Diploma
  - Accreditation

- After graduation
    - Counseling (further studies, job opportunities)
    - Further education offers (postgraduate programs or similar)

Rekkedal and Qvist-Eriksen (2011) found out that the feedback on assignments submitted was the most important issue for students, followed by the access to a tutor and online tutorials. The possibility to contact other students had the lowest level in the study.

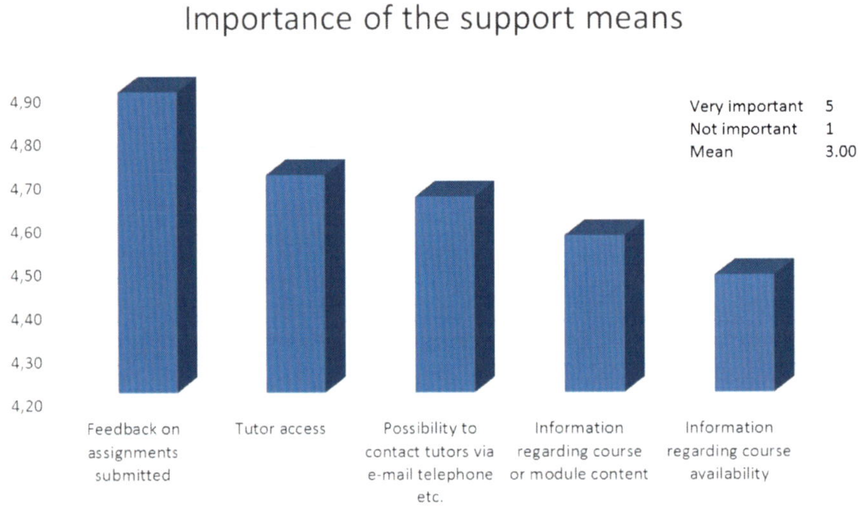

Figure 19: The Top Five (student activities in Blended Learning)

4.2. Blended Learning Course Activities

Blended Learning course should be planned, structured, designed, and executed in a learner-centered way. The course itself should use competence oriented learning outcomes. Consequently, the teaching method and the definition of the course leads to students that are involved more actively in the learning process.

Learner-centered teaching is defined as active learning and students' engagement, which involves students in the learning process. The teachers or trainers attend the student being the center of the learning activities. The teachers and trainers work as facilitators, tutors, guides or simply as specialists in the taught subject.

Corley (2012) describes in the TEAS Center Fact Sheet #6

> *Student-centered learning is an approach to learning in which learners choose not only what to study but also how and why. At the heart of the learning environment are learner responsibility and activity, in contrast to the emphasis on instructor control and coverage of academic content found in conventional, didactic teaching.*

The learner-centered activities affect the learner as well as the trainers and as the learning itself.

For the **learners** a learner-centered access means to be active in their learning and to make decisions about what and how they will learn. They construct new knowledge and skills on current knowledge and skills; they are intensively involved in collaborative work with other learners (in groups). They reflect what they are learning; they are motivated by their input in group work and their contributions to joint projects. All this can be done in onsite teaching as well as in the distance learning (based on technology).

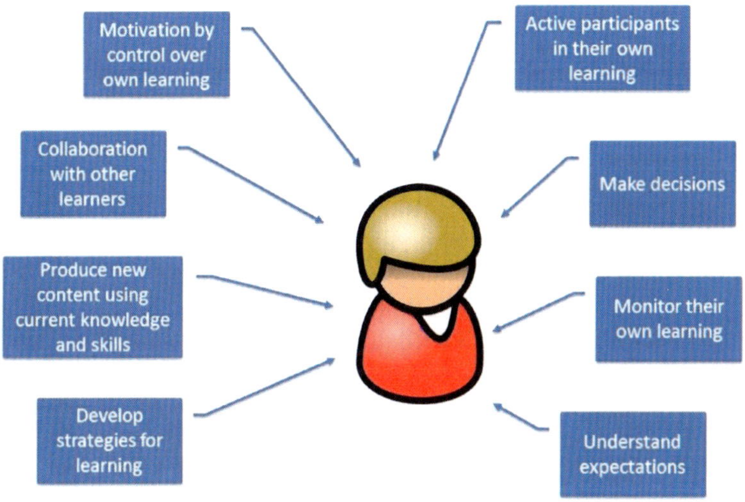

Figure 20: The learner in a learner-centered environment

The **teachers and trainers** have to encourage and facilitate the learners during the learning process, they help the learners to work through difficulties and to study and solve problems. They facilitate discussions in learners' groups and provide the necessary knowledge without overruling the students' work. All of that can also be managed in onsite teaching as well as in the distance learning.

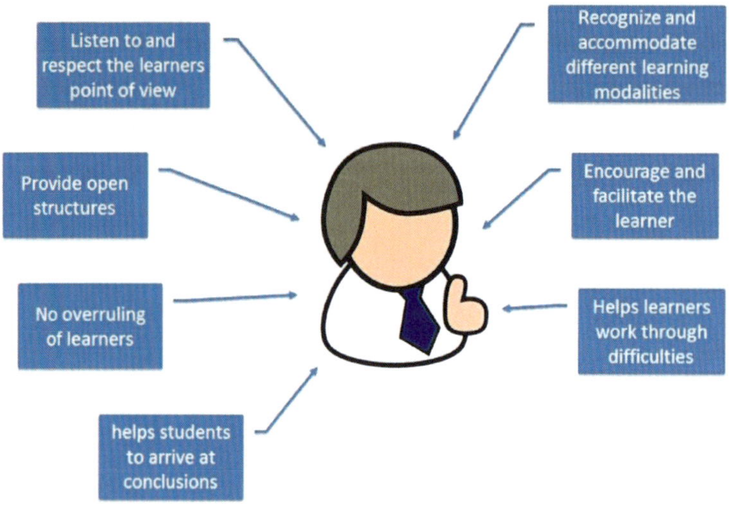

Figure 21: Teacher in a learner-centered environment

A learner-centered Blended Learning environment causes various preconditions in the instructional strategies and methods. The main issues are

- A flexible time management to satisfy and match learners' needs
- To provide peer learning as well as collaboration in small groups
- To provide an appropriate support for learners and developing and using effective learning strategies for each task.
- More responsibility for the learner during the learning process, especially in the distance learning
- To provide tasks, questions and assignments that encourage the learner's thinking
- To provide tasks and activities that are personally relevant to learners
- The use of critical thinking skills to refine the learner's understanding

The process of moving to learner-centered teaching is often not easy for older teachers. In this case, a well-prepared further education is necessary to bring the teachers near to the new teaching methods.

The learner-centered access to teaching is a key to create, perform and execute the various activities described below. The following chapters describe a selection of teaching activities, their possible use and a short statement in context with the quality framework (if necessary).

Typical quality criteria in a quality framework is always a strict decryption about the topic, expected outcomes or products, timeframes and support options.

4.2.1. Collaboration and cooperation

Brindley, Walti and Blaschke (2009) note that learner-learner interactions in an eLearning course can be viewed as a four-stage continuum (that is valid for Blended Learning courses as well):

1. **Communication**

   People talking to each other - are discussing

2. **Collaboration**

   People sharing ideas and working together (occasionally sharing resources) in a loose environment

3. **Cooperation**

   People doing things together, but each with his or her own purpose

4. **Community**

   People striving for a common purpose

4.2.2. Readings

Readings or the use of textbooks are classical distant learning tools. Teachers should keep in mind that reading can provide knowledge, but cannot be counted to active teaching methods.

Use in Blended Learning

For Blended Learning, a combination of reading with other activities is recommended. Bonk and Khoo (2014, p. 9) present reading as a part of the read - reflect - display - do model. The first phase of the model emphasizes reading, listening and text-based activities.

4.2.3. Writing

Writing is an active learning tool as it forces learners to work out answers systematically and actively. Writing activities can take a number of forms. Furthermore, writings are a method of individualized teaching. An additional effect is to strengthen the mother tongue.

Use in Blended Learning

Writing as an activity makes sense especially in the distance-learning phase.

4.2.4. Lectures

Lectures are a classical means of onsite teaching. Recording special lectures in a special environment can also be used in the online phase. Teachers should keep in mind that video-recorded lectures do not count to active learning; they only can be part of an activity.

It is important for teachers to know that lectures in general are less learner-centered teaching activities. From the point of economical learning, it can be considered that lectures still have their place in the teaching area if the lecturer can involve the students actively in the lesson.

Use in Blended Learning

Video-recorded lectures do not count to active learning; they only can be one part in a learning activity - for example as a teaser, knowledge base or impact to critical thinking.

Special quality criteria are necessary to create a valuable video. In the same way, the use of videoed lectures must be considered from the quality point of view.

4.2.5. Expert guests

Expert guests are an enrichment - especially if they are available for discussions with learners or if they are directly involved in group-learning activities.

Use in Blended Learning

Expert guests are extremely useful in onsite teaching. In the online teaching, it depends on the technical environment to create a reasonable learning activity. One method is to use a webinar to present the expertise of a guest to the learners. That requires a high level of technical equipment.

It is recommended evaluating the balance of the expenditure to the use for the learners.

4.2.6. Simulations

A simulation simulates a real-world situation. Simulations can be used in a twin way in teaching:

1. A simulation (or simulation program) is used to give learners the possibility to experiment with different parameters special issues of the reality.
2. The other way is to let the students create an artificial representation of real conditions (either in computerized or in print form).

Use in Blended Learning

Simulations can be used in onsite learning as well as in online teaching. In most cases, a special software is used for the simulation itself. That causes that the students are familiar with this software (that implies for students to practice the use of the software).

A quality criterion in that context is the strict planning of practicing the use of the software, optional to check license problems and to provide the necessary support.

4.2.7. Role play

There are different reasons for role-plays and access methods. The aim of this activity (in most cases) is to focus learners' attention to a specific problem and to perform creative solutions.

A group of students will be asked to take on the parts of characters in a representation of a real situation. This is similar to a case study, but with added character descriptions. This activity is effective for practicing managerial skills, language teaching or topics with a personal impact to the participants.

Use in Blended Learning

There are several options. A group can develop the storyboard with the characters online and perform the realization in the onsite teaching. Another option is that each learner prepares him or herself to the topic and executes an off-the-cuff performance leading to a peer discussion.

Role-plays can be used in onsite teaching as well as in online teaching or as a combination.

4.2.8. Case studies

A group of students is given a narrative description of a problematic situation and then they are asked to identify or solve the problem. Students are provided with background information.

The teacher/trainer describes a problem and questions are asked. Students explore "what if" situations and expand the case or come to some conclusions. Case studies can be seen as an intensive active learning.

Use in Blended Learning

Case studies can be used in onsite teaching as well as in online teaching.

Important are

a) The group work and
b) The active input of all group members.

4.2.9. Video/Web Analyses

The interesting activity in context with a video or a web analyses is the writing of the reflection or the summarizing of findings. The analyses are typical individual activities, supplemented by additional activities, which can be group activities as well.

Use in Blended Learning

The method of video or web analyses is an impulse for further activities. The typical environment is the online phase. A combination with individual presentations of the findings during the onsite phases is a nice combination.

A quality criterion is the delivery of the video. That must be planned in a learner-friendly way.

4.2.10. Research modules or investigations

That can be either a single student activity or a group activity. The result must be presented in an adequate way.

Use in Blended Learning

The activity can be used either in the onsite teaching or in the distance learning. A mixture of investigations in the distance learning combined with an onsite presentation makes sense.

A quality criterion is a well-planned and properly developed concept for such combined activities. A context to the instructional design exists here.

4.2.11. Brainstorming

This activity is highly associated with creative methods. In learner-centered teaching, it is a typical group activity realized with various methods (typical brainstorming in onsite teaching; joint development of a mind map in distance learning).

Use in Blended Learning

The various methods of brainstorming are useful in both phases of Blended Learning.

A quality criterion is the good preparation of used tools, especially in the distance learning.

4.2.12. Individual presentation

Individual presentations are an appropriate method for individual assignments or assessments. A good addition is a peer review with a discussion, maybe combined with a forum (in the distance learning).

Use in Blended Learning

Presentations as well as peer reviews can be organised in the onsite teachings as well as in the distance learning.

4.2.13. Debate teams

Debates are a means of encouraging critical thinking, personal expression, and tolerance of others' opinions. Good topics contain authentic concerns, multiple perspectives, controversy, and real-world impact.

Use in Blended Learning

Debates are activities, which are useful in onsite teaching as well as in online teaching.

The connected quality criterion is a technical issue: It is suggested to provide the essential tools for the execution of the debates in online teaching.

4.2.14. Structured group projects

In these group projects, the learners compare and contrast perspectives; they practice high-level cognitive skills (i.e., application, analysis, synthesis, evaluation) and have to develop meta-skills such as leadership, communication, conflict resolution. Furthermore, they have to strategize and plan how to tackle complex problems and distribute work in the group

Use in Blended Learning

Structured group projects are a well-tested and experienced activity, which can be used either in onsite teaching or in distance learning. They require facilitating by trainers and should have an appropriate defined ending, like a final presentation or some other valuable outcome.

A quality criterion is a well-done description of the complete activity including the goals, the provided support, the expected competences and learning outcomes and finally the type of assessment.

4.2.15. Individual student project

These activities are similar to the structured group projects; however, the learners do an individual work. They have to explore areas of interest in depth; to conceive of, to plan and to execute a research or creative project from beginning to end. They work independently and seek mentorship from an expert in the field or other research resources. Trainers facilitate the learners during the project.

Use in Blended Learning

Individual student projects are a well-tested and experienced activity, which can be used either in onsite teaching or in distance learning. They require facilitating by trainers and should have an appropriate defined ending, like a final presentation or some other valuable outcome.

They offer the option of an individual final assessment for the attended course.

4.2.16. Collaborative discussions

Collaborative discussions are an imperative strategy for enhancing understanding, clarifying and refining meaning, making connections and synthesizing knowledge. They practice thinking and communicating in the subject or discipline. In the same way, it is possible to evaluate positions, arguments, or designs as well as to defend an own position. In these discussions it is possible to identify problems, conflicts and inconsistencies and to get feedback from (or even about) students. The results often draw on students' expertise and prior knowledge.

Use in Blended Learning

Collaborative discussions should be conducted in onsite teaching. Therefore, they stay alive, are exciting and thrilling and give a direct impact to all involved students. From the practical experience in teaching at a high school, the author does not advise to use that activity in distance learning.

An interesting option is to use one of the learners to moderate the discussion; as a result, the teacher can concentrate on the learners' observation. This leads to the student-led discussions.

A quality criterion is the careful preparation of the environment. The discussion environment covers the venue where the collaborative discussion takes place, the definition of the necessary frame conditions like the used time and the precise topic)

For effective learning, it is necessary to balance the peer interaction.

4.2.17. Student-led discussions

This activity is typical for the distance learning. It is a suitable way to develop leadership skills and to learn (and to reflect) a topic in the learning process in a different way.

For teachers it is necessary to keep in mind that the moderation of an online discussion may be extremely time consuming. Another issue is the quality of the moderator - low quality makes the other learners suffer.

Use in Blended Learning

Student-led discussions can be performed in onsite teaching as well as in distance learning. Balancing the problem of time consuming with the possible learning success will influence you to select another activity method. Besides, the group factor is low in distance learning.

A quality criterion is to provide the technical environment for the discussions.

4.2.18. Instructor-led group discussion

This is a similar method as the student-led discussion. The equality of the students in the participation group makes the difference. Besides that, it is a well-proved method for individualisation in the teaching and learning process.

Use in Blended Learning

Instructor-led group discussions can be implemented in onsite teaching as well as in distance learning. In online teaching, it is more difficult to keep students engaged and to keep them actively involved in a lively discussion. Therefore, this activity often leads to failures in reaching the goals.

A quality criterion is to provide the technical environment for the discussions.

4.2.19. Labs/Studies

The focus of labs (for example computer labs) or studies is to develop disciplinary and process skills. Students should obtain immediate feedback and respond to it.

During the lab lessons, students should develop metacognitive skills (e.g., awareness of own strategies) and should learn to evaluate results or product of own work. With their experience, they should also be able to approximate real life situations.

Use in Blended Learning

Labs are a typical onsite teaching activity and usually need a high level of students' support. Studies with no need of expansive technical equipment or other related items may be conducted in distance learning too.

A quality criterion is the state of the art (technical) equipment for the lab; another is the strict, precise and all-embracing instruction for the learner.

4.3. Course Development Step by Step

Good praxis in Blended Learning requires only some basic considerations and must pursue few basic principles.

The best strategy to develop a blended course is to start at zero level - it is not advisable to try to change an existing course by dedicating some learning activities to the distance learning and to leave everything unchanged.

There are many theories about teaching and learning. You have to decide for a suitable method in teaching that fits perfectly to your institution as well as to your future students.

A modern access to teaching should use learner-centered methods and competence oriented learning outcomes.

The next step is to define the used quality framework - on institutional level or - for small organisations - hand-tailored to the course.

A very good guide for developing Blended Learning courses (Blended Learning Implementation Guide Version 2.0, 2013[17]) was published by the American Initiative "Digital Learning Now"[18].

The author plans a special book with the practical implementation of Blended Learning courses using the developed framework within the next year.

4.4. Concepts for a Quality Framework in Blended Learning

A quality framework provides a certain form and structure for the quality assurance. In most cases, they focus to bring a structure to processes to which they are applied. Many frameworks are built from the point of view of the school,

---

[17] N.N. (Ed.) (2013): Blended Learning Implementation Guide. Digital Learning Now, http://digitallearningnow.com/site/uploads/2014/05/BLIG-2.0-Final-Paper.pdf, checked on 05/17/2015.

[18] http://digitallearningnow.com/

university, course or training provider. Moreover, the learner and the learner's needs are included as well in the presented framework.

The quality framework is a kind of reference source and can be seen as a kind of toolkit that can be used in many ways to improve the quality in teaching and learning. Typical for quality frameworks is the fact that they do not completely prescribe the quality processes, but they channel processes in a specific direction that accords to the best praxis. Another issue is that not all items must be relevant for the specific course or for a training institution,

Quality frameworks in Blended Learning can be seen as versatile guidelines. The responsible person of an organisation has to adapt and to concretise the quality framework to the institutional quality plan describing the affected issues and the involved processes - the responsibilities as well as the evaluation methods based on measurable facts or descriptions.

4.4.1. Basic considerations for a quality framework

For many decades, quality in teaching was measured and characterised as teacher (or institution) centered. The continuous development in teaching methods and praxis led to a learner-centered access (Anderson 2008, p. 311). The new paradigm measures can be seen as learner-centered and with a special focus on the learner and the learners' needs. The new and partly innovative access to a quality framework should care about issues like deferential access to competences, tailored and open teaching, collaborative methods, and flexibility in teaching, learning and collaboration. Furthermore, learning-as-constant with time-as-variable, teacher-skilled, aggregated experience, learner-driven motivation; international/global oriented knowledge, dynamic acting and learning, distributed delivery model in teaching, competence oriented (learning) outcomes, and optimised services (Anderson 2008, p. 311).

4.4.2. Principle of the quality assurance

There is a discussion in literature about the principles used in quality assurance: process versus outcomes (Anderson 2008, p. 321). A versatile access to quality management should care for both. In this book, the learners' needs are also included in the considerations of quality management.

The presented quality framework describes each quality criteria (as a part of a specific quality field) by a simple table, where the quality manager can assign the necessary answers to four basic questions.

In this book, this table is added at the end of the description or considerations and compiled with proposals or examples for an all-purpose Blended Learning environment. These proposals can be replaced by more strictly descriptions in the context of the developed course.

The four basic questions for quality management are:

1. What is the main quality objective for the mentioned process (activity)?
2. Who are the responsible actors (responsibility)?
3. Which methods or instruments can be used to assure quality (tools)?
4. How can we measure the success of the quality objective (indicators)?

4.4.3. Key principles of the presented quality framework for Blended Learning

The presented framework includes various key principles. They build a kind of basement for all described quality fields, quality criteria and responsibilities.

- Provision of effective and efficient administrative services
- Informed planning and resource management
- General access for all leaners including individualisation in teaching
- Appropriate (instructional) design, development and implementation of teaching for effective and active learning (learner-centered access)
- Providing of well-educated staff at the current level of knowledge familiar with the necessary teaching competences
- Maintaining, managing and facilitating the technical infrastructure (at a current level of technology)
- Evaluation of the teaching environment as a permanent process
- Understanding of the requirements and desires of learners
- Support of the learners´ needs

4.4.4. Possible structure

This book offers a framework using five columns as a basement for the quality assurance. These columns derive from the basic considerations done in chapter three. They all include an access to quality following the idea of following the student's needs.

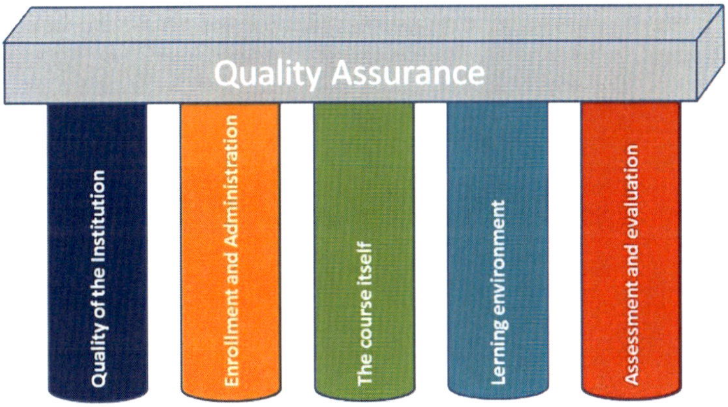

Figure 22: Columns of the quality framework

4.5. The Quality Framework

The quality framework uses the results of the Grundtvig Multilateral Project "Blended Learning Quality-Concepts Optimized for Adult Education" 539717-LLP-1-2013-1-IT-GRUNDTVIG-GMP, which complements the ideas and research results used in this book. Additional impact results from literature and the research experience of the author done in the field of Blended Learning praxis.

For each column, the main quality criteria are mentioned in a general way completed by mentioning of possible actors, methods and instruments and the measures of success.

The descriptions give an overview for the main issues. They may be seen as examples how such a quality framework can be defined and implemented.

4.5.1. Quality of the institution

A well-organised institution should have a mission and a vision of their position in the teaching landscape. Additional, there exist policy statements. Action plans and finally activities, which enable to fulfil the organisation´s mission and vision.

Quality objective for the mentioned process	The institution determines its own mission and objectives that reflect its academic commitments and the needs of society.
Responsible actors	Head, steering committee or similar organisational structure in the teaching institution
Methods or instruments to assure quality	Quality circle (plan - act - check - do) for continuous evaluation and improvement
Measure the success of the quality objective	Questionnaire to students and other stakeholders with best feedback, interview with stakeholders with positive feedback

Table 6: General quality assignments of the institution

It is advisable for an institution to provide a stated policy with regard to quality assurance and monitoring in all aspects of its operations. That causes the implementation of a quality framework covering organisational as well as academic activities of the institution.

Quality objective for the mentioned process	Implementation of a quality framework in all fields of the organisation (administration, teaching)
Responsible actors	Quality manager
Methods or instruments to assure quality	Corporate/Strategic plan; internal quality assurance teams, interaction with staff and students
Measure the success of the quality objective	Feedback on various ways (questionnaires, interview, focus groups)

Table 7: Implementation of a quality framework

The institution has a policy for the effective use of Information and Communications Technology (ICT) in support of distance education, deliver content and supply the teaching activities.

Quality objective for the mentioned process	Use of ICT in teaching (relevant for students as well as for teachers/trainers)
Responsible actors	Head, scientific committee, teachers
Methods or instruments to assure quality	Strict integration of the use of ICT in all areas of administration and instructions
Measure the success of the quality objective	Student and teacher feedback proves a high level of ICT integration

Table 8: ICT as a general quality issue

The institution cares for state of the art equipment and for the best technical and human resources. Teachers and trainers are well educated and qualified for teaching in onsite environments as well as in distance learning.

Quality objective for the mentioned process	Provide high quality in both technical and human resources
Responsible actors	Head, scientific committee
Methods or instruments to assure quality	Job descriptions, regularly continuous education of teaching and trainer staff
Measure the success of the quality objective	Student and teacher feedback proves a high level of technical equipment and teacher education

Table 9: Equipment in the institution

4.5.2. The enrolment

The institution provides a clear policy for all enrolment topics - that covers the information about all related course issues as well as the appropriate administrational background.

Quality objective for the mentioned process	Enrolment policy
Responsible actors	Administration
Methods or instruments to assure quality	Regularly checks of the enrolment, feedback from students
Measure the success of the quality objective	Positive feedback of students

Table 10: Enrolment and administration in the institution

The institution offers a clear information policy covering the preconditions to attend a course especially in ICT knowledge, the use of the distance learning, the special settings and the learning effort.

Quality objective for the mentioned process	Information policy
Responsible actors	Administration, (pedagogical) head
Methods or instruments to assure quality	Documents and information material (with regularity monitoring, adaption and necessary amendments)
Measure the success of the quality objective	Positive feedback of students

Table 11: Information policy in the institution

The institution provides comprehensive information about the selected course including the preconditions, potential preparation activities, the expected student group (size, age, pre-knowledge) and other relevant course facts.

Quality objective for the mentioned process	Provide an optimised course information
Responsible actors	Administration, (pedagogical) head
Methods or instruments to assure quality	Documents and information material (with regularity monitoring, adaption and necessary amendments)
Measure the success of the quality objective	Positive feedback of students

Table 12: Course information policy

4.5.3. The course itself

There are precise learning objectives and the course is structured in competence oriented learning outcomes. The competence oriented learning outcomes are well- defined. The course concept cares for a well-defined structure of the course with appropriate split of activities and teaching to the onsite and distance learning.

Quality objective for the mentioned process	Definition of the learning activities and the different parts of onsite and online teaching
Responsible actors	Administration, (pedagogical) head
Methods or instruments to assure quality	Documents and information material, rubrics and tables with teaching activities, learning outcomes, timetables
Measure the success of the quality objective	Learning objectives and outcomes are well-defined and can be evaluated easily

Table 13: Course information

The specifications of the course describe the coverage of the course, the prerequisite knowledge, key instructional techniques that will be used and the methods for the various assessments.

Quality objective for the mentioned process	Detailed and explicit course description including pre-knowledge, instruction methods, and assessment methods
Responsible actors	Administration, (pedagogical) head
Methods or instruments to assure quality	Documents and information material
Measure the success of the quality objective	Students expect prior knowledge and competences have been considered, key aspects of the course and learner context have been researched and specified, clear statements about the teaching and assessing of learners are available

Table 14: Course information

The students' interaction with course material as well as the interaction between students are a key factor in learner-centered learning. Therefore, the course material should be relevant, appropriate and clear. The material is sufficiently tested, logically structured and sequenced. This is valid for the onsite teaching as well as for the distance learning.

Quality objective for the mentioned process	Well-planned and structured course materials with interactions between students.
Responsible actors	(pedagogical) head, course creator
Methods or instruments to assure quality	Documents and information material, feedback from students as well as from trainers (or teachers)
Measure the success of the quality objective	The content is well structured and provides interactions between students. There are clear study routes through the course Positive feedback of students

Table 15: Course structure and student's interactions

Students may expect materials at a high level and - if possible (and necessary) - including a mixed media set. Material should be created using a good graphic design and be accessible by good interfaces (with various devices). The materials should offer a variety of different activities with a widespread mix of methods. This is valid for onsite and distance learning.

Quality objective for the mentioned process	Good technical design of materials
Responsible actors	Course creators; people are responsible for the teaching materials
Methods or instruments to assure quality	Document descriptions, checklists
Measure the success of the quality objective	Learning materials (and other teaching contents) are designed to work efficiently in the provided course environment

Table 16: Teaching materials

Activities for the students should be provided in a well-designed method mix and distributed to the onsite teaching as well as to the distance learning.

Quality objective for the mentioned process	Students' activities
Responsible actors	Pedagogical head, course developer
Methods or instruments to assure quality	Course design External evaluation
Measure the success of the quality objective	Students feedback shows a high level of satisfaction External evaluation proves a well-structured activity pool

Table 17: Students' activities

The course structure including the various activities keeps students engaged and cares for a reasonable learning success of the students.

Quality objective for the mentioned process	Students engagement
Responsible actors	Course design, involved teachers
Methods or instruments to assure quality	Observation from students, tracking control of the students' activities
Measure the success of the quality objective	Students' feedback prove satisfaction during the learning process

Table 18: Students' engagement

4.5.4. The learning environment

The learning environment consists of the physical learning and teaching environment during the onsite teaching and the learning platform in the distance learning. Both learning and teaching situations are equally and the course provider must care for the relevant quality in both settings.

Modern, well-equipped classrooms with the option to split easily into smaller groups are necessary. In the same way, the technical equipment as projectors, optimised lab structures or electrical infrastructure should be taken for granted.

Quality objective for the mentioned process	Quality of the onsite teaching environment
Responsible actors	Administration, pedagogical head
Methods or instruments to assure quality	Regularly research creating checklists for equipment and environment
Measure the success of the quality objective	Students' feedback proves a high level of satisfaction

Table 19: Onsite teaching environment

The course offers a well-equipped learning platform providing the necessary features, tools and options for successfully teaching in a learner-centered setting.

Quality objective for the mentioned process	Quality of the learning platform
Responsible actors	Administration, pedagogical head, technical staff
Methods or instruments to assure quality	Regularly research creating checklists for equipment and environment Checklists for features and tools of the platform
Measure the success of the quality objective	Students' feedback proves a high level of satisfaction Teachers' feedback does the same

Table 20: Quality of the eLearning platform

Communication and collaboration is a well-established process in the course structure.

Quality objective for the mentioned process	Communication and collaboration
Responsible actors	Course designer, teachers and trainers, students
Methods or instruments to assure quality	Precise description of the necessary collaboration structure between students Well defined communication guidelines including the description of technical issues
Measure the success of the quality objective	Feedback from the students proves their satisfaction Teachers' feedback is related to the defined expectations

Table 21: Communication and collaboration

The learning platform is not only used in the distance learning. It is a tool for administration, providing materials, and works as a repository as well as it builds a connectivity bridge between the students and between students and trainers. That gives a high priority level to the selection of a well-fitting learning platform.

The findings of the study in the frame of the "Blended Learning Quality" Grundtvig project dealing with learning platforms showed a lack of learning platforms (as open source software) fulfilling the expectations and needs in the distance learning (Consortium Blended Learning Quality 2015)

Quality objective for the mentioned process	Learning platform tools and features
Responsible actors	Research group of the teaching institution, technician
Methods or instruments to assure quality	Checklist with the features and tools
Measure the success of the quality objective	Percentage of the hits in the checklist

Table 22: Learning platform tools

A crucial issue in Blended Learning is the tutorial support, especial in the distance learning.

Quality objective for the mentioned process	Adequate tutorial support for the learners
Responsible actors	Trainers, technical support of the institutions
Methods or instruments to assure quality	Description of the possible tutorial support
Measure the success of the quality objective	Students' feedback can be used to measure the satisfaction with the received feedback, facilitation and support by the trainers (or teachers)

Table 23: Tutorial support for students

4.5.5. Assessment and evaluation

Assessment as an integral part of teaching is necessary to prove the learners' success. Assessment is useful for students as well as for teachers. Student assessment should be considered as summative as well as formative activities. Peers, teachers or other usual assessment tools and practices can do that.

The best solution is a continuous assessment, so teachers and students can easily estimate the learning success. Assessment methods must be available in the onsite teaching as well as using the learning platform. The students receive a timely feedback about their assessment results.

Quality objective for the mentioned process	Assessment settings
Responsible actors	Trainers
Methods or instruments to assure quality	Well-defined descriptions of the assessment and the assessments' goals Continuous assessment during the course in both learning forms
Measure the success of the quality objective	Students' assessments are an integral part of the course design Students have the opportunity to verify their learning progress Assessment is used as a monitoring tool for the ongoing learning progress Timely feedback is given to the students

Table 24: Assessment

To measure the course quality various methods can be used. In any case, some evaluation of the course (organisation, teachers' quality) as well as the learning outcomes of the students must be provided. That can be done by the usual evaluation methods. A detailed description of the used methods must be published at the course start. Results must be published in a qualified way to the students. The organisation must use a qualified assessment circle to provide a continual course improvement.

Quality objective for the mentioned process	Evaluation of the course
Responsible actors	Administration, teachers, learners
Methods or instruments to assure quality	Well-described monitoring and evaluation processes Use of tracking facilities of the learning platform Feedback from students Course reviews and analyses
Measure the success of the quality objective	Course material and design are reviewed regularly There is evidence of appropriate response to the reviews There exist appropriate feedback mechanism to support the course improvement and further development of the course

Table 25: Course evaluation

5. Evaluation and Validation

The evaluation of Blended Learning courses is part of the developed quality framework. Blended Learning is a relatively new teaching method because of its combination of onsite teaching and distance learning. Therefore, it is not surprising that in literature there cannot be found any relevant study comparing the learning effectiveness of online and face-to-face teaching (Means 2009, p XII) from 1996 through 2006.

Ni (2013, pp. 201) compares the effectiveness of onsite and online learning. She compares institutional issues like the learning environment as well as learner related matters like interactions of students. In her findings, she mentions a higher level of effectiveness in the online teaching, but a significant higher importance of the teaching in the classroom. That study demonstrates that the evaluation of Blended Learning courses is a multidimensional undertaking with a complex background.

Quality assurance is undoubtedly a purpose of evaluation and deeply connected to the used quality framework. Dyson and Campello (2003 pp. 12) describe the needs of evaluation and focus on five purposes of evaluation. They develop a framework for the evaluation of virtual learning environments. Some of their findings are still relevant for Blended Learning courses. Especially the definition of engagement (of students), participation and achievement of goals are still a fact in modern evaluation strategies.

5.1. Definitions

The following chapter distinguishes between evaluation and validation. The reason is to develop a system, in which the learner gives feedback of the course from the special view of the learner (and the learner's needs).

5.1.1. Understanding of evaluation of a Blended Learning course

Evaluation can be defined as the systematic assessment of the worth or merit of some objects. Evaluation can be self-evaluation described as "The act or result of judging the worth or value of something or someone"[19].

---

[19] The American Heritage® Roget's Thesaurus. Copyright © 2013, 2014 by Houghton Mifflin

There are different types of evaluation, depending on the objects being evaluated. Formative evaluation focuses on the usability of the object (Blended Learning course as a product). One of the goals is to detect and to eliminate usability problems.

Theofanos (2005 p 29) describes special formative testing methods and defines formative testing as testing with representative users and representative tasks on a representative product, in which the testing is designed to guide the improvement of future iterations.

Summative evaluation measures performance and/or satisfaction goals of a complete Blended Learning course. The aim is to judge to the degree of fulfilment of a course after the complete course is performed or conducted. Results of the summative evaluation should be used for amendments. To be contrary to formative evaluation (which focuses on the usability or a process), the summative evaluation cares about the results by comparing defined expectations with the reached outcomes.

Kurilovas and Dagiene (2012 pp 143) offer an interesting summary of various evaluation methods developed for distance learning. These methods could be useful to be considered as a part in the evaluation strategy of a Blended Learning course as well.

Frydenberg (2002) mentions five aspects of course design in distance education: learning goals and content presentations; interactions; assessment and measurement; instructional media, tools, learner services and support. This basically meets some of the quality fields developed by the consortium of the BladEdu project (2013).

5.1.2. Understanding of validation of Blended Learning

The free dictionary defines validation - "the act of validating; finding or testing the truth of something" and offers the term "proof" as a synonym[20]. That targets the general understanding of validation as it was used in the Grundtvig Multilateral Quality in Blended Learning Grundtvig Project (Consortium Blended Learning Quality 2015).

Harcourt Publishing Company. Published by Houghton Mifflin Harcourt Publishing Company.

[20] American Heritage® Dictionary of the English Language, Fifth Edition. Copyright © 2011 by Houghton Mifflin Harcourt Publishing Company. Published by Houghton Mifflin Harcourt Publishing Company. All rights reserved.

The access of validation is to find an answer to the question: "How did the course improve my skills?" or "How useful was the course for me / were the in the course developed or improved skills (for my further development / for my job or other related issues) ".

5.1.3. Self-evaluation

Self-evaluation is a method deriving from business and is used to describe and consider the performance of employees. Self-evaluation leads to become active in the evaluation process as well as it serves to increase commitment to goal achievement and competency development.

Tilkin (2009, p. 9) defines self-evaluation as

> *Self-evaluation of education and/or learning is the process of systematic collection, analysis and exchange of data concerning educational processes of either individuals, groups or organisations (institutions, etc.) in order to facilitate learning among all parties concerned so value judgments and decision-making may be based on evidence rather than on intuition.*

The method of self-evaluation is an appropriate tool for both teachers and students. Tilkin (2009, p. 7) mentions that self-evaluation enables dialogue between all parties concerned in teaching and learning. In this book, the method of self-evaluation is mainly described as a means for students to evaluate their learning progress and experience.

5.2. What Should be Evaluated?

The target of the evaluation of a Blended Learning course should be the course itself as well as the learner´s satisfaction. Course evaluation can be done easily by a good planning including the evaluation issues in the concept of the course. The developed quality framework should be used for formative and summative evaluation.

Graham (2013, p. 342) mentions that learner satisfaction is a complex issue often depending on the environment, mood, expectations, goals and preferences of the learner. Student´s satisfaction is connected to learner dispositions as well as to course design. That is proved by Dos (2014), who found out that students reported their satisfaction with the interactive content.

Kurilovas and Dagiene (2012, p. 142) use the terms "internal quality" and "quality in use" as their evaluation targets.

5.3. Preparation

Van Lakerveld (2011 p 10) recommends to set the first steps to a powerful and appropriate evaluation in the pre-course phase. Therefore, the evaluation fields including the necessary indicators must be defined during the course development.

To plan an effective and appropriate evaluation, various accesses are possible.

5.4. Course Evaluation using the Framework

An appropriate and well-proofed method for evaluation is the use of rubrics. Quality Matters[21] promotes the use of rubrics and offers tables with standards for the evaluation[22]. Each of the general standards (in Higher Education 8 general standards are foreseen) can be measured with up to 3 points, the sum provides as a numeric value an information of the course quality.

In conformity with the developed five quality fields of the framework, five rubrics can be used to evaluate the course.

The developed and used rubrics describe for each quality field the quality criteria with a brief description and the possible indicators. The possible answer can be chosen out from a Likert-Scale. (Four values from excellent ↔ bad) This type of evaluation offers an intensive multi-level interpretation. Mazohl (2015) published a versatile method of numeric-based analyses and interpretations including a basic customers´ satisfaction interpretation.

The published rubrics must be seen as a sample how evaluation can be defined and performed using the developed framework. As this book describes versatile environments and courses, the framework is more or less an all-purpose proposal and must be adapted to the specific organisations, courses and maybe to the taught subjects too.

5.4.1. The institutions quality

Frydenberg (2002) mentions the institutional commitment as a standard domain for quality assurance.

---

[21] Quality Matters is a non-profit organization involved in quality assurance in Online Education, https://www.qualitymatters.org/

[22] As an example here is the link to the Higher Education rubric standards https://www.qualitymatters.org/node/2305/download/QM%20Standards%20with%20Point%20Values%20Fifth%20Edition.pdf

Topic		Indicators
Administration	**Technical administration**	The institution has an identified group of key staff responsible for formulating, evaluating, developing and executing data of students.
		The Blended Learning strategy is part of the general educational strategy of the institution.
		Appropriate operating and security standards especially providing online services as well as student's data are defined.
	Program Administration	Activities will be linked with the institution's processes and defined quality assurance system for a continuous improvement (based on monitoring, feedback and self-evaluation of involved staff).
		Appropriate policy guidelines and processes are installed to ensure the correct participation of students at the teaching activities (including assessments).
Documentation		The institution provides appropriate guidelines for the documentation of the course as well as for the documentation of the students.
		The institution provides the necessary policy for privacy of students.
Resources	**Technical**	The institution cares for the necessary technical equipment
	Human	Appropriate guidelines exist to ensure that sufficient qualified teachers are available for the course (onsite teaching as well as for the tutorial support).

Topic		Indicators
	Financial	The institution cares for the necessary financial resources to ensure all enrolled students to finish the course.
Teachers/Trainers	**ICT Skills**	The teachers who are involved in the course hold the necessary ICT knowledge to conduct the course and to teach the students with missing ICT knowledge.
	Didactic Skills	The institution has the policy to use teachers with the necessary didactic skills to perform the specific teaching activities.
Instructional		The institution cares for appropriate definitions of the specifications of the course in context with a Blended Learning structure of the course

Table 26: Indicators for the institution's quality

5.4.2. The enrolment

The enrolment procedure is an integrant of starting a course. In an appropriate quality framework, the enrolment must be described properly and the institution has to supply the learner with all necessary and evident information. This covers the various processes of the proper enrolment procedure, the provided course information and other related issues. An overview of indicators is summarized in the following table.

Topic		Indicators
Students´ inform	**Available information**	The institution's policy provides sufficient and comprehensive course descriptions
		The institution cares for individual solutions depending on the students' situation

Topic		Indicators
		The institution provides the necessary description for the environment of the course
	Enrolment procedure	The institution's policy provides a clear and well documented enrolment process
		The institution provides a policy to assist students during the enrolment process.
Students´ preparation		The institution provides a general policy to inform and support students in the necessary preparation work for the course.
		The institution provides a general policy for necessary entrance assessments and the consequences.
Students´ group		The institution provides a general policy to create well-fitting students´groups for the courses (number of students, personal environment of students)

Table 27: Indicators for quality in the enrolment

5.4.3. The course itself

Brindley and Walti (2009) describe in their findings the need to establish a healthy balance between structure (clarity of tasks) and learner autonomy (flexibility of tasks). Self-paced learning, especial in the distance learning, can enable that.

They recommend the establishment of learner relationships and a sense of community to perform efficient group work - an important issue for the onsite teaching as well as for the distance learning. The positive effects mentioned above can be realised by including small group collaborative learning experience in Blended Learning courses.

Topic		Indicators
Course planning		The course structure is planned in context with the institution's policy
Students´ activities		There exists a clear description for students about the expected student activities during the course.
		The distance learning components provide a range of learning experience for students and are adequately interactive.
Students´ expectations		The institution provides appropriate descriptions of the course (organisation, content) to provide the necessary information to the students.
Split the learning outcomes		The curriculum provides an appropriate mixture of online and onsite teaching (based on competence oriented learning outcomes)
Technology		The used technology is clearly described in the course information and available for all students.
		There exists a clear policy in the institution how students can be supplied in technical issues to ensure a successful participation at the course.
Engage students		The instructional design of the course foresees methods and learning activities to engage students in the learning process.

Topic		Indicators
Teachers´ behaviours		The institution provides the necessary information about the students for teachers and trainers to perform an optimised course schedule.
		The description of the course defines a practicable support of the learners by the teachers and makes the importance of this support clear to the teachers
		The institution provides the necessary educational support for the students.
Duration of the course		The curriculum provides an appropriate time management and schedule for the course, which gives the students the time frame to fulfil the assignments and to tackle the learning amount.
Definition of goals and learning outcomes	**Competence oriented learning outcomes**	The course description defines clear and reasonable competences, which are taught by the course.
		The course description defines clear and reasonable learning outcomes.
Learning approach		The course description defines clear and reasonable access methods for the various activities foreseen during the course.

Topic		Indicators
		The course description provides appropriate and well-defined tutorial support for students.
		The institution cares for learning interaction between individuals and within groups, for social interaction between students and students and makes clear and transparent in which collaborative activities students' participation is required.
		The course description defines an appropriate approach to learning (the priority should always be a learner-centered approach).
Evaluation of course and student performance	**Onsite learning**	The course description defines clear and reasonable assessment methods to evaluate the students' performance
		The course description defines clear and reasonable assessment results to evaluate the students' performance
	Distance learning	The course description defines clear and reasonable assessment methods to evaluate the students' performance
		The course description defines clear and reasonable assessment results to evaluate the students' performance
		There exist criteria for the assessment of students´ online collaboration and they are applied constantly during the course.

Topic		Indicators
Teaching tasks		The course description defines clear and reasonable teaching tasks
Multimedia		The course concept provides and describes the intensive use of multimedia in the teaching activities.

Table 28: Indicators for the course

5.4.4. The learning environment

Brindley and Walti (2009) describe the challenge of creating effective study groups. They mention the theory of connectivism, developed by George Siemens (Siemens 2005), and explain the learning in the digital age relying on the connected learning that occurs through interaction with various sources of knowledge and group tasks.

The learning environment of a Blended Learning course has to provide all these features - in the onsite teaching as well as in the distance learning.

Technology plays an important role in the onsite teaching as well as in the distance learning.

Topic		Indicators
The modern classroom		The institution provides a comfortable, well-equipped and structured learning environment (mainly rooms) well-fitting to active learning using a learner-centered access to teaching.
		Learners are supplied in time with the full information on sequence, timing and duties within their intended program of study.

Topic		Indicators
Communication and Collaboration		The technical equipment provides various individual and group-based communication tools.
		The system provides the necessary collaboration tools for effective group work (and assessment too).
LMS and VLE		The availability, the function and the purpose of all learning materials are clearly defined and communicated to students.
		Provided material is well-performed for self-paced learning.
		Course materials and components have a consistent and stringent user interface with unified styles, common formats etc.
		Course materials and the technical delivery system are tested (in realistic conditions in pilot sessions).
On-site Activities and Quality		The distance learning system is appropriate for the course requirements and supports all defined students activities.
		The VLE supports rich interactivity
Distance Learning Activities and		The technical infrastructure is well defined and supports all foreseen teaching activities.
		The system meets the equipment and connectivity requirements of student users.

Table 29: Indicators for the learning environment

5.4.5. The assessment and evaluation

The assessment can be seen as a feedback how the students are doing in their effort to reach the learning outcomes. From that understanding, feedback is always goal-oriented. Assessment should be done continuously in a formative approach using all the activities performed by the students. In some cases, a summative assessment may be necessary - in many cases, it is done if the students get a diploma or a certificate. Students should be assessed using published criteria, regulations and procedures, which are applied consistently.

The necessary course evaluation is split into two essential parts: Course evaluation and evaluation of the learning success of the students.

The course evaluation should include on one hand the course itself and on the other hand the teaching (including teaching quality of teachers and trainers).

Topic		**Indicators**
Assessment and testing definitions		Assessments for students (summative and formative) are appropriate implemented as an integral part of the course design
		The course design cares for sufficiently and timely opportunities for students to verify their progress towards achieving learning objectives.
		Adequate and well defined measures are implemented in the course to ensure objectivity and consistency in giving marks or giving feedback to the students.
		The course development defines continuous assessment activities split into different activities in the course.
Learning outcomes		Assessments are implemented in the course development to evaluate the defined learning outcomes.

Topic		Indicators
		Assessments are implemented in the course development to evaluate the defined competences taught by the course.
Evaluation and Feedback		The course is monitored regularly.
		Feedback from students and trainers is used for continuous and longer term improvements.
		Students and trainers are actively involved in the evaluation process of the course.
		There are appropriate descriptions for the quality enhancement and improvement of the course (in context with the evaluation)
		The teaching quality is evaluated (minimum once)
Assessments		The course provides appropriate assessment methods
		Learners are well informed about the assessment conditions before and about the results after the assessment.

Table 30: Evaluation and assessment

5.5. Additional Considerations

The evaluation of a course is often seen as an individual and single process (Frydenberg 2002). In modern teaching, the process of evaluation starts with the definition of the course goals and competence oriented learning outcomes and ends with the feedback from the students and the teachers/trainers. That means that evaluation can only be done in a permanent running process during the course. Course improvements or amendments can be the result of an analysis of the permanent evaluation. Here a "lessons learned" session of the trainers is useful and will bring the necessary amendment proposals.

To develop a final questionnaire for the evaluation of a Blended Learning course it is necessary to be aware of the evaluation goal. Using a quality framework, it is necessary to set the focus of the evaluation on special issues of the course. The evaluation strategy should be part of the description of the quality framework.

In the literature, you may find several interesting access methods for an evaluation strategy. Here are some examples for other quality frameworks, which can be used in Blended Learning.

5.5.1. Five Pillars (Online Learning Consortium, former Sloan Consortium)

The framework focuses on five areas of evaluation, namely the learning effectiveness, scale (cost effectiveness and commitment), access, faculty satisfaction and students´ satisfaction. It describes the goals of each of these elements and discusses some possible metrics.

5.5.2. CoI Community of Inquiry Survey Instrument

The community of Inquiry questionnaire was developed and validated by a collaborative research team (Arbaugh 2008). The information about the system is hosted at the webpage of the Athabasca University in Canada[23].

5.5.3. Ten questions to evaluate Blended Learning courses

The Free University Berlin provides ten significant questions in their online questionnaire about Blended Learning. These questions focus on

- The information before the course,
- The preparation of the students,
- The content of the course was explained to students properly,
- The information and preparation of assignments,
- The final work with results of assignments,
- The clear and strict description of goals and results of online activities,
- The appropriate use of media in the course,
- The students' success of learning,

[23] https://coi.athabascau.ca/coi-model/coi-survey/

- The efficiency of the teaching mixing onsite and distance teaching, and
- The desire of the students to have more courses based on Blended Learning.

The questions of this questionnaire can be used for the quality framework developed in that book too.

5.5.4. Blended Learning Toolkit[24]

The University of Central Florida (2015) provides a Blended Learning Toolkit. They offer questionnaires for students and for faculty. The material resumes from 2011 and mentions the use of web based services.

[24] N.N. (2015): Survey Instruments | Blended Learning Toolkit. University of Central Florida (UCF). Available online at https://blended.online.ucf.edu/evaluation-resources/survey-instruments/, checked on 7/2/2015.

6. Conclusion

Is there any reason why Blended Learning is a kind of current trend?

Hoffman (2006) gives an interesting impact:

> *In part, it makes significant economic sense that even the beans-counters can see immediately; Blended Learning also makes sense due to the emergence of geographically dispersed work environments in which staffing levels are constantly being changed.*

In the meantime, Blended Learning can be named as an established teaching method.

6.1. Relevance of Blended Learning

Vlachos (2010) presented a research project comparing face-to-face teaching with Blended Learning (the taught subjects were foreign languages). The study was conducted with students from three European countries (aged 10 - 11). In two tests, the groups were evaluated and compared.

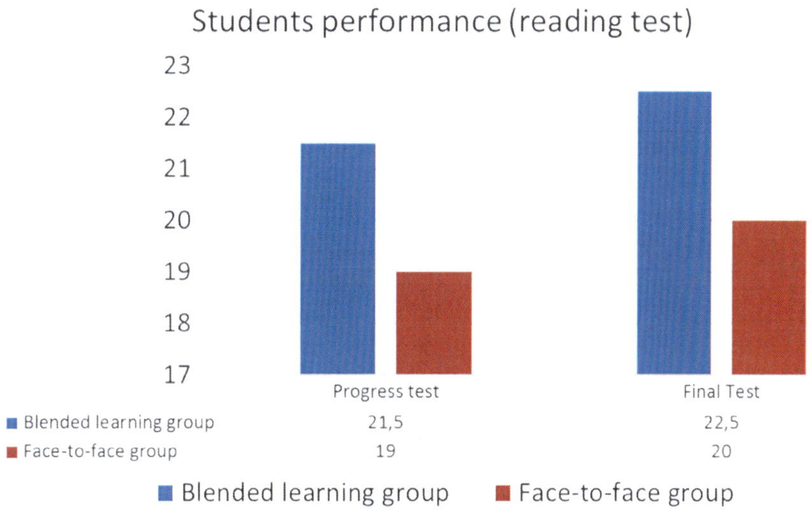

Figure 23: Performance comparison in language teaching (face-to-face teaching vs blended learning)

Obviously, the Blended Learning group does better. As a reason Vlachos mentions:

> *It can, therefore, be supported that the systematic online communication the blended learning students experienced, the methodical use of the word processor with its syntax and grammar control, the interactive-publishing online platform of communication, where they could instantly upload and download multimodal electronic materials, and, last but not least, the face-to-face guidance they received from their teacher and peers strengthened their communicative reading and writing skills.*

The mentioned facts (from the EFL experience) demonstrate that Blended Learning is an efficient and successful teaching method, which will play a more important role in the future.

Moritz (2008) describes a study performed in Graz to proof that existing onsite teaching can be switched to Blended Learning courses.

Watson (2015, p. 10) also proves in a study, that teaching in Blended Learning systems is more successful compared with traditional teaching systems. The study shows a percentage of higher scoring in reading, mathematics and science in the range of +19 % up to +27 %.

There are many examples being found in literature. What is absolutely missing is an appropriate concept or well-defined framework for quality assurance.

6.2. Why Quality Frameworks are Necessary

EdisonLearning (2015) defines a quality framework as „a research-based descriptive and evaluative tool that covers all that teachers do in and out of classrooms to enable great learning."

A quality framework must be more: It must cover the quality assurance of the complete teaching and learning activities, furthermore the learning environment and the connected process - as the enrolment - as well.

Ehlers (2007) defines quality in eLearning as

> *... an imperative for practitioners, and a huge demand for learners. Achieving high quality is a much debated and sought-after goal in all segments of education.*

Additional, the learners' needs also must be an issue in quality frameworks,

That would address to the distance learning, but can be expanded to the complete teaching and learning processes. He recommends the professionalization of quality development, especial the increasing of technological deficits. This is addressed to both learner and teacher.

A quality framework in Blended Learning must cover the field of quality assurance as well as the quality enhancement. It should be used to foster quality improvements in the teaching institution.

The Consortium Quality in Blended Learning (2014) proposes to foresee measures in the quality framework to care for the learners´ needs in the learning environment as well.

6.3. Future Development and Further Steps

The presented quality framework is the first step to quality assurance, quality improvement and quality enhancement in Blended Learning. It was developed theoretically out from studies, and got a huge impact from the participation at the Grundtvig Multilateral Project about Quality in Blended Learning[25] (2013). The framework developed in that project was enhanced, completed and commented.

The next steps must be to develop pilot courses and to implement the framework in an appropriate way. The courses should be part of qualified scientific studies. A proper evaluation and analyses can be used to proof the functionality of the framework and to care for necessary amendments and improvements in the framework's definition.

The same way, the subjects of the courses should be varied and evaluated seriously.

Watson (2015) mentions in the publication of the iNACOL[26] that

> *Blended learning is not about the technology itself; it is about the shift in the instructional model to personalized, student-centered learning to ensure each student's success.*

This can be seen as an invitation in further qualified research to refine the very successful teaching method of Blended Learning.

---

[25] Grundtvig Multilateral Project "Blended Learning Quality-Concepts Optimized for Adult Education" (BLAdEdu) 539717-LLP-1-2013-1-IT-GRUNDTVIG-GMP.

[26] International Association for K–12 Online Learning, http://www.inacol.org/

References

Ableidinger, Joe; Han, Jiye Grace; Hassel, Bryan C.; Hassel, Emily Ayscue (2013): A Better Blend: A Vision for Boosting Student Outcomes with Digital Learning. Public Impact. Chapel Hill, NC. Available online at http://opportunityculture.org/wp-content/uploads/2013/04/A_Better_Blend_A_Vision_for_Boosting_Student_Outcomes_with_Digital_Learning-Public_Impact.pdf, checked on 8/16/2014.

Albrecht, Bob (2006): Enriching Student Experience Through Blended Learning. ed. ECAR (Educause Review, 12). Available online at https://net.educause.edu/ir/library/pdf/ERB0612.pdf, checked on 4/15/2015.

Allen, I. Elaine; Seaman, Jeff; Garrett, Richard (2007): Blending in: The Extent and Promise of Blended Education in the United States. In Sloan Consortium (NJ1). Available online at http://files.eric.ed.gov/fulltext/ED529930.pdf.

Anderson, Terry (2008): Theory and practice of online learning. 2nd ed. Edmonton: AU Press.

Angelino, Lorraine (2007): Running head: ENGAGE STUDENTS AND REDUCE ATTRITION RATES. In The Journal of Educators Online 4 (2), checked on 2/26/2015.

Anthony F. Grasha (1994): A Matter of Style: The Teacher as Expert, Formal Authority, Personal Model, Facilitator, and Delegator. In College Teaching 42 (4), pp. 142–149, checked on 4/9/2015.

Arbaugh, Cleveland-Innes et al. (2008): CoI Survey | CoI. Athabasca University. Available online at https://coi.athabascau.ca/coi-model/coi-survey/, checked on 7/2/2015.

Asen, Karin, M.A (2013): E-Learning - Hype oder Flop? Bestandsaufnahme und Zukunft des E-Learnings. Available online at http://www.dieberater.com/fileadmin/downloads/dieBerater-E-Learning-InterviewAsen-DRUCK_7-1-13.pdf, checked on 8/20/2014.

Aycock, Alan; Garnham, Carla; Kaleta, Robert (2002): Lessons Learned from the Hybrid Course Project. In Teaching with Technology Today 8 (6). Available online at http://www.uwsa.edu/ttt/articles/garnham2.htm, checked on 10/26/2014.

Barclay, Kathleen (2003): The Live e-learning cookbook. Recipes for success. New York: IUniverse.

Battaglino, Tamara Butler; Haldeman, Matt; Laurans, Eleanor (2012): Creating Sound Policy for Digital Learning. The Costs of Online Learning. In Creating Sound

Policy for Digital Learning, pp. 1–14. Available online at http://www.edexcellencemedia.net/publications/2012/20120110-the-costs-of-online-learning/20120110-the-costs-of-online-learning.pdf, checked on 6/8/2015.

Bersin, Josh (2004): The blended learning book. Best practices, proven methodologies, and lessons learned. San Francisco, CA: Pfeiffer (Essential resources for training and HR professionals).

Bloom, Benjamin S. (1972): Taxonomie von Lernzielen im kognitiven Bereich. Weinheim: Beltz (Bettz Studienbuch).

Board of studies (2015): Advice on Assessment. Board of studies, teaching & educational standards. Board of Studies New South Wales. Australia. Available online at syllabus.bos.nsw.edu.au/assets/global/files/advice_on_assessment_guide_web.pdf, updated on 2015, checked on 4/26/2015.

Bonk, Curtis Jay; Graham, Charles Ray (Eds.) (2006): The handbook of blended learning. Global perspectives, local designs. 1st ed. San Francisco: Pfeiffer (Pfeiffer essential resources for training and HR professionals).

Bonk, Curtis Jay; Khoo, Elaine (2014): AAdding some TEC Variety. 100+ Activities for Motivating and Retaining Learners Online. 1st ed. 1 volume. Bloomington, Indiana, USA: Open World Books, checked on 2/5/2015.

Bostes (2015): see Board of studies (2015)

Brannen, Ivy (2014): LibGuides. EDUC 4475: Clinical Internship. Effective Teaching & Learning. Savannah State University Library. Available online at http://savannahstate.libguides.com/content.php?pid=648061&sid=5365743, checked on 4/11/2015.

Breitenecker, Felix; Körner, Andreas; Winkler, Stefanie (2014): AKMATH. Institut für Analysis und Scientific Computing, UT Vienna. Available online at http://akmath.tuwien.ac.at/, checked on 11/3/2014.

Brindley, Jane E.; Walti, Christine; Blaschke, Lisa M. (2009): Creating Effective Collaborative Learning Groups in an Online Environment. In *The International Review of Research in Open and Distributed Learning* 10 (3). Available online at http://www.irrodl.org/index.php/irrodl/article/view/675/1271, checked on 2/5/2015.

Chen, Baiyun; Denoyelles, Aimee (2013): Exploring Students' Mobile Learning Practices in Higher Education. University of Central Florida (Educause Review).

Available online at http://www.educause.edu/ero/article/exploring-students-mobile-learning-practices-higher-education, checked on 4/15/2015.

CIIA (2014): CIIA: Teaching and Learning Resources. Western Washington University. Available online at
http://pandora.cii.wwu.edu/cii/resources/outcomes/how_assessment_works.asp, updated on 4/26/2015, checked on 4/27/2015.

Clayton Christensen Institute (Ed.) (2012): Blended Learning Model Definitions | Christensen Institute. Clayton Christensen Institute. Available online at
http://www.christenseninstitute.org/blended-learning-definitions-and-models/, updated on 8/20/2014, checked on 8/20/2014.

Commission, European: Aid Delivery Methods - Project Cycle Management Guidelines Vol 1 - Guidelines. DG International Cooperation and Development. Available online at
https://ec.europa.eu/europeaid/sites/devco/files/methodology-aid-delivery-methods-project-cycle-management-200403_en_2.pdf, checked on 4/27/2015.

Consortium Blended Learning Quality (2015): Project Summary. With assistance of Harald Makl, Luca Reitano. Edited by Peter Mazohl. Consortium Blended Learning Quality. Available online at
http://www.blendedlearning-quality.net/typo3/index.php?id=7, checked on 5/10/2015.

Corley, Mary Ann (2012): TEAL Center Fact Sheet No. 6: Student-Centered Learning | Teaching Excellence in Adult Literacy (TEAL). Available online at
https://teal.ed.gov/tealguide/studentcentered, updated on 9/4/2014, checked on 2/4/2015.

Dell, Cindy Ann; Low, Christy; Wilke, Jeanine F. (2010): Comparing Student Achievement in Online and Face-to-Face Class Formats. In JOLT - Journal of Online Learning and Teaching 6 (1). Available online at
http://jolt.merlot.org/vol6no1/dell_0310.htm, checked on 11/3/2014.

Deva, Mukul (2013): FCUK Your Way to Success Breakthrough Leader - Minimum Effort. Maximum Result. Energize Yourself. Empower Others. Transform Performance Effortlessly // The art of maximising results with minimum effort. Singapore: Marshall Cavendish Editions.

Dillenbourg, Pierre: Virtual learning environments. Workshop on Virtual Environments. In: EUN Conference 2000 proceedings. Available online at http://tecfa.unige.ch/tecfa/publicat/dil-papers-2/Dil.7.5.18.pdf, checked on 4/17/2015.

Donnelly, Roisin (2010): The Nature of Complex Blends: Transformative Problem-Based Learning and Technology in Irish Higher Education. In Yukiko Inoue (Ed.): Cases on online and blended learning technologies in higher education. Concepts and practices. Hershey PA: Information Science Reference.

Dos, Bulent (2014): Developing and Evaluating a Blended Learning Course. In *Anthropologist* 17 (1), pp. 121–128, checked on 4/17/2015.

Dublin, Lance (2008): Web 2.0 and Learning 2.0 Leading to Innovation 2.0. In Innovation & Enterprise Agility Advisory Service 2 (11). Available online at http://www.lancedublin.com/blog/documents/CutterLearningInnovationDublin.pdf, checked on 10/24/2014.

Dyson, Mary; Barreto Campello, Silvio (2003): Evaluating Virtual Learning Environments: what are we measuring? In The Electronic Journal of e-Learning 1 (1), pp. 11–20, checked on 4/18/2015.

EdisonLearning (2015): Quality Framework for Learning and Teaching. Available online at http://edisonlearning.net/what-we-offer/quality-framework-for-school-development/quality-framework-for-learning-and-teaching.html, checked on 5/1/2015.

Ehlers, Ulf (2007): Quality Literacy — Competencies for Quality Development in Education and e-Learning. In *Educational Technology & Society* 10 (2), pp. 96–108, checked on 4/21/2015.

ENQA (2009): Standards and guidelines for quality assurance in the European Higher Education Area. Helsinki: European Association for Quality Assurance in Higher Education (ENQA report on standards and guidelines for Quality Assurance in the European Higher Education Area, [8]). Available online at http%3A//www.worldcat.org/oclc/76853320, checked on 4/15/2015.

Faust, Jennifer L.; Paulson, Donald R. (1998): Active Learning in the College Classroom. In Journal on Excellence in College Teaching 9 (2), pp. 3–25, checked on 2/3/2015.

Fischer, Ewald Guido (1995): 10 Jahre Informatik an den AHS. Eine große Weichenstellung für die Zukunft. In COMPUTER KOMMUNIKATIV (6), pp. 6–11. Available online at http://pubshop.bmukk.gv.at/download.aspx?id=553, checked on 6/8/2014.

Friesen, Norm (2012): Report: Defining Blended Learning. Associate Professor in Educational Technology, Boise State University. Available online at [Web] http://learningspaces.org/papers/Defining_Blended_Learning_NF.pdf.

Froyd, Jeff; Simpson, Nancy (2008): Student-Centered Learning (SCL). Student-Centered Learning Addressing Faculty Questions about Student-centered Learning. Texas A&M University. Available online at http://ccliconference.org/files/2010/03/Froyd_Stu-CenteredLearning.pdf, checked on 1/25/2015.

Frydenberg, Jia (2002): Quality Standards in eLearning: A matrix of analysis. In *The International Review of Research in Open and Distributed Learning* 3 (2).

Garrison, D. Randy; Vaughan, Norman D. (2008): Blended learning in higher education. Framework, principles, and guidelines. 1st ed. San Francisco: Jossey-Bass (The Jossey-Bass higher and adult education series).

Gejel, Jan (2010): The role of ICT in Grundtvig courses. Available online at http://www.ginconet.eu/sites/default/files/library/The%20role%20of%20ICT%20in%20Grundtvig%20courses.pdf, checked on 10/25/2014.

GINCO Grundtvig International Network for Course Organisers (2014): Welcome to the GINCO website | Grundtvig International Network of Course Organisers. Alden Biesen. Available online at http://www.ginconet.eu/home, checked on 10/26/2014.

Ginns, Paul; Ellis, Robert (2007): Quality in blended learning: Exploring the relationships between on-line and face-to-face teaching and learning. In The Internet and Higher Education 10 (1), pp. 53–64. DOI: 10.1016/j.iheduc.2006.10.003.

Graham, Charles R. (2013): Emergencing practice and research in Blended learning. In Michael G. Moore (Ed.): Handbook of distance education. 3rd ed. New York: Routledge, pp. 333–350.

Grasha, Anthony F. (1994): A Matter of Style: The Teacher as Expert, Formal Authority, Personal Model, Facilitator, and Delegator. In College Teaching 42 (4), pp. 142–149, checked on 4/9/2015.

Guy, Monica (2013): Structured vs. unstructured online learning - eLearning for all. Edited by Monica Guy. eLearning for all. Available online at http://elearningtransforms.com/structured-vs-unstructured-online-learning/, checked on 5/15/2015.

Heinze, Aleksej; Procter, Chris; Coates, Nicola (2004): Reflections On The Use Of Blended Learning // Education in a changing environment. Scholarship, educational research and development at the University of Salford: proceedings of the University of Salford's 2nd Learning and Teaching Research Conference 13th -14th September 2004. Salford: University of Salford, checked on 10/20/2014.

Hofmann, Jennifer (2014): 101 Tips To Motivate the Virtual Learner. InSync Training. Available online at http://www.insynctraining.com/pages/101TipsToMotivatetheVirtualLearner.pdf, checked on 4/9/2015.

Hoic-Bozic, Natasa; Mornar, Vedran; Boticki, Ivica (2009): A Blended Learning Approach to Course Design and Implementation. In IEEE Trans. Educ. 52 (1), pp. 19–30. DOI: 10.1109/TE.2007.914945.

Horn, Michael B. (2012): Is the 'Technology' Ready for Blended Learning? Innosight Institute. Available online at http://www.blendmylearning.com/2012/11/16/is-the-technology-ready-for-blended-learning/, checked on 10/22/2014.

http://www.elearnspace.org/Articles/connectivism.htm, checked on 2/7/2015.

Johnston, Jerome; Barker, Linda Toms (2002): Assessing the Impact of Technology in Teaching and Learning: A Sourcebook for Evaluators. In Institute for Social Research, University of Michigan. Available online at http://www.rcgd.isr.umich.edu/tlt/TechSbk.pdf, checked on 2/4/2015.

Körner, Andreas; Winkler, Stefanie: AKMATH. Blended Learning Auffrischungskurs Mathematik der TU Wien. Analysis und Scientific Computing, UT Vienna. Available online at http://akmath.tuwien.ac.at/index.php?id=44, checked on 11/3/2014.

Kurilovas, Eugenijus; Dagiene, Valentina (2010): Multiple Criteria Evaluation of Quality and Optimisation of e-Learning System Components. In *Electronic Journal of e-Learning* 8 (2), pp. 141–151, checked on 4/18/2015.

Lorenzo, George; Ittelson, John (2005): An Overview of E-Portfolios. In EDUCAUSE Learning Initiative (ELI), pp. 1–27. Available online at https://net.educause.edu/ir/library/pdf/eli3001.pdf.

Mann, Sarah J. (2004): Guidelines for Writing Aims and Intended Learning Outcomes at the Programme and Course level. University of Glasgow. Available online at https://www.ied.edu.hk/obl/files/pratical_guide_1.pdf, checked on 1/25/2015.

Mayer, Richard E. (2001): Multimedia learning. Cambridge, New York: Cambridge University Press.

Mazohl, Peter (Ed.) (2014): Quality issues for blended learning courses focusing on the learner. Quality in Blended Learning. Wiener Neustadt, 20/02 - 22/02. EFQBL:

BladEdu Consortium. Available online at http://www.blendedlearning-quality.net/typo3/fileadmin/user_upload/project_results/pdf/02%20Quality-Criteria-Details_V-01.pdf, checked on 2/12/2015.

Means, Barbara (2009): Evidence-Based Practices in Online Learning: A Meta-Analysis and Review of Online Learning Studies -- May 2009 (PDF). With assistance of Yukie Toyama, Robert Murphy, Marianne Bakia, Karla Jones. Edited by Center for Technology in Learning. U.S. Department of Education. Available online at https://www2.ed.gov/rschstat/eval/tech/evidence-based-practices/finalreport.pdf, checked on 4/16/2015.

Mishra, R. C. (2009): Educational research. New Delhi: A.P.H. Pub. Corp.

Moriz, Werner (2008): Blended learning. Entwicklung, Gestaltung, Betreuung und Evaluation von E-Learningunterstütztem Unterricht. 1. Aufl. Norderstedt: Books on Demand.

Ni, Anna Ya (2013): Comparing the Effectiveness of Classroom and Online Learning. In Journal of Public Affairs Education 19 (2), pp. 199–215. Available online at http://www.naspaa.org/jpaemessenger/Article/VOL19-2/03_Ni.pdf, checked on 1/25/2015.

Niegemann, Helmut M.; Domagk, Steffi; Hessel, Silvia (2007): Kompendium Multimediales Lernen. Dordrecht: Springer (X.media.press).

Pappalardo, Lucia; Gunn, Cindy (2013): Utilizing active learning strategies to enhance learning in Chemistry-Case Studies. In Learning and Teaching in Higher Education: Gulf Perspectives 10 (1), checked on 2/3/2015.

Pawlowski, Jan M. (2007): The Quality Adaptation Model: Adaptation and Adoption of the Quality Standard ISO/IEC 19796-1 for Learning, Education, and Training. In Educational Technology & Society 10 (2), pp. 3–16.

Precel, Karen; Eshet-Alkalai, Yoram; Alberton, Yael (2009): Pedagogical and Design Aspects of a Blended Learning Course. In International Review of Research in Open and Distance Learning 10 (2).

Prensky, Marc (2001): Digital Natives, Digital Immigrants Part 2: Do They Really Think Differently? In The strategic planning resource for education professionals 9 (6), checked on 1/25/2015.

Prinsloo, Paul (2009): Modelling Throughput at Unisa: The key to the successful implementation of ODL in ODL Communication and Task Team Reports. Available online at http://hdl.handle.net/10500/6035, checked on 4/26/2015.

Rekkedal, Torstein; Qvist-Eriksen, Svein (2011): Support Services in E-Learning - an Eevaluation Study of Students' Needs and Satisfaction. Available online at http://www.eurodl.org/materials/contrib/2004/Rekkedal_Qvist-Eriksen.htm, updated on 11/2/2011, checked on 2/4/2015.

Rosell-Aguilar, Fernando (2007): Top of the Pods—In Search of a Podcasting "Podagogy" for Language Learning. In *Computer Assisted Language Learning* 20 (5), pp. 471–492. DOI: 10.1080/09588220701746047.

Sarria, Aline; Molina, Elizabeth Carrandi (2012): An Innovation Sensation: Shifting Charter Schools from traditional to Blended Shifting charter schools from traditional to Blended Learning Models, checked on 10/22/2014.

Sehra, Siddharth; Maghu, Sunakshi; Bhardawaj, Avdesh (2014): Comparative Analysis of E-learning and Distance Learning. In International Journal of Information & Computation Technology 4 (8), pp. 823–828. Available online at http://www.irphouse.com/ijict_spl/ijictv4n8spl_07.pdf, checked on 10/24/2014.

Siemens, George (2005): Connectivism: A Learning Theory for the Digital Age. In *elearn space*. Available online at

Smythe, Michael (2011): blended-learning-a-transformative-process. Nelson Marlborough Institute of Technology. Available online at https://akoaotearoa.ac.nz/download/ng/file/group-3740/smythe---blended-learning-a-transformative-process.pdf, checked on 10/16/2014.

So, Hyo-Jeong; Brush, Thomas A. (2008): Student perceptions of collaborative learning, social presence and satisfaction in a blended learning environment: Relationships and critical factors. In Computers & Education 51 (1), pp. 318–336. DOI: 10.1016/j.compedu.2007.05.009.

Springer Gabler Verlag (Ed.) (2014): Gabler Wirtschaftslexikon, Stichwort: Blended Learning, online im Internet. Available online at http://wirtschaftslexikon.gabler.de/Archiv/435569391/blended-learning-v5.html, updated on 10/20/2014, checked on 10/20/2014.

Stacey, Elizabeth; Gerbic, Philippa: Success factors for blended learning. In : Ascilite 2008 Melbourne, pp. 964–968.

Staker, Heather Clayton; Horn, Michael B. (2012): Classifying-K-12-blended-learning. Innosight Institute. Boston. Available online at http://www.christenseninstitute.org/wp-content/uploads/2013/04/Classifying-K-12-blended-learning.pdf, checked on 10/22/2014.

Stein, Jared; Graham, Charles R. (2014): Essentials for blended learning. A standards-based guide. New York: Routledge (Essentials of online learning series).

Tabor, Sharon W. (2007): Narrowing the Distance. Implementing a Hybrid Learning Model for Information Security Education. In The Quarterly Review of Distance Education 8 (1), pp. 47–57. Available online at http://robinwofford.wiki.westga.edu/file/view/24958021.pdf/238607251/24958021.pdf, checked on 8/6/2014.

Talluri, Shalini (2013): The Expectations of Learners, Trainers and Managers from an LMS. Edited by Dr. Ayesha Habeeb Omer. CommLab India LLP,. Available online at http://blog.commlabindia.com/lms-hosting/customization-of-lms.

The Centre for Teaching Excellence (Ed.) (2014): Blended learning. University of Waterloo. Available online at https://uwaterloo.ca/centre-for-teaching-excellence/resources/blended-learning, updated on 10/16/2014, checked on 10/16/2014.

Theofanos, Mary; Quesenbery, Whitney (2005): Towards the Design of Effective Formative Test Reports. In *Journal of Usability Studies* 1 (1), pp. 27–45, checked on 4/17/2015.

Thorpe, Mary (2002): Rethinking Learner Support: the challenge of collaborative online learning. In Open Learning: *The Journal of Open, Distance and e-Learning* 17 (2), pp. 121–137. DOI: 10.1080/02680510220146887.

Tilkin, Guy (Ed.) (2007): Self evaluation in adult Life Long Learning. With assistance of Jaap Van Lakerveld, Selma van der Haar. Alden Biesen: Grundtvig Project SEALL, Guy Tilkin, checked on 4/16/2015.

TUWEL (2014): TUWEL-Kurs | ZIDline | Zentraler Informatikdienst | TU Wien. University of Technology, Vienna (ZID). Vienna. Available online at http://www.zid.tuwien.ac.at/zidline/zl18/tuwel_kurs/, checked on 10/24/2014.

University of Central Florida (2015): Design and Delivery Principles | Blended Learning Toolkit. University of Central Florida. Available online at https://blended.online.ucf.edu/effective-practices/design-delivery-principles/, checked on 7/4/2015.

University of Central Florida (2015): Types of Courses at UCF | Online@UCF. Edited by University of Central Florida. University of Central Florida. Available online at http://online.ucf.edu/learn-online/types-of-courses-at-ucf/, updated on 1/24/2015, checked on 1/24/2015.

van Lakerveld, Jaap; Zoete, Joost de (2011): GINCO: Quality in courses. PLATO. Edited by Jaap van Lakerveld. Ginco Grundtvig International Network for Course Organisers. Leiden. Available online at http://www.ginconet.eu/sites/default/files/GINCO_Grundtvig_Course_Quality_tool_EN.pdf.

Vaughan, Norman D. (2007): Perspectives on Blended Learning in Higher Education. In International Journal on E-Learning, 6(1), pp. 81–94.

Vaughan, Norman D.; Cleveland-Innes, M.; Garrison, D. R. (2013): Teaching in blended learning environments. Creating and sustaining communities of inquiry. Edmonton: AU Press (Issues in distance education series).

Vlachos, Kosmas (2010): Comparing face-to-face with blended learning in the context for foreign languages. In Ng, Eugenia M. W. (Ed.): Comparative blended learning practices and environments. Hershey, PA: Information Science Reference, pp. 250–274.

Watson, John (2008): Promising Practices in Online Learning: Blended Learning - The Convergence of Online and Face-to-Face Education. Edited by John Watson. iNACOL, checked on 5/12/2015.

Watson, John (Ed.) (2015): Blending Learning: The Evolution of Online and Face-to-Face Education from 2008–2015. With assistance of Allison Powell, John Watson, Patrick Staley, Susan Patrick, Michael Horn, Leslie Fetzer, Laura Hibbard, Jonathan Oglesby, Su Verma. iNACOL. Vienna: iNACOL, checked on 7/12/2015.

Wiley, David (2015): Edited by David Wiley. Lumen Learning. Available online at http://davidwiley.org/, updated on 6/29/2015, checked on 6/30/2015.

Yee, Kevin (2012): Interactive Techniques. Loyola Marymount University. Available online at http://www.lmu.edu/Assets/Centers+$!2b+Institutes/Center+for+Teaching+Excellence/interactive+teaching+techniques+pdf.pdf, checked on 10/26/2014.

Glossary

Accessibility includes more or less technical aspects.

Accessibility
Defines the extent to which a course is designed to allow disabled students to take part at the learning activities. The W3C[27] consortium declares, “it is essential that the Web be accessible in order to provide equal access and equal opportunity to people with diverse abilities.”

Availability
It defines the percentage of time in which a service - like an eLearning course - is available for the user and not unavailable due to failure, technical problems or other events (for example schedules maintenance activities).

Blended Learning
Blended Learning (in the context of this book) is defined as a mix of (minimum) two different teaching methods or learning praxis. Typically, it is combined of a face-to-face teaching (onsite teaching) and online learning.

Case Study
A way of learning about a complex instance through extensive description and analysis. The case study articulates why the instance occurred as it did by exploring the factors contributing to its success or failure, and what one might consider in similar situations.

Checklist
A checklist is a predefined set of guidelines, tasks, or other items against which products, processes, behaviors, user interface components, or something else, are compared.

Cloud Computing
The practice of using a network of remote servers hosted on the Internet to store, manage, and process data, rather than a local server or a personal computer.
A way of using computers in which data and software are stored or managed on a network of servers (= computers that control or supply information to other

[27] World Wide Web Consortium (W3C), http://www.w3.org/

computers), to which users have access over the Internet (The Oxford Dictionary, 2015).

Course

It means a well-defined unit of teaching with no fixed duration. Courses provided by university normally last for a semester.

ELearning platform

An eLearning platform is a framework of tools that work seamlessly together to deliver a student centric learning experience by unifying educational theory & practice, technology and content. ELearning platforms usually are hosted on a web server and are accessed by using the Internet.

ELearning

ELearning means a learning method facilitated with ICT. ELearning does not necessarily means learning by the Internet; the "e" normally stands for the three keywords "everywhere", "every time" and "electronically".

European Association for Quality Assurance in Higher Education

The **European Association for Quality Assurance in Higher Education[28] (ENQA)** is an umbrella organisation, which represents quality assurance organisations from the European Higher Education Area (EHEA) member states.

Evaluation

Means the making of a judgement about the amount, number, or value of something. Evaluations assess items, services, organisations or other issues to create a comparable value. In education, evaluation means the systematic appraisal of the effectiveness of teaching or learning.

Feedback

Commentaries, advices and recommendations given to students on examinations or assessments are called feedback. Normally feedback is given by the teacher or trainer. Feedback can also be given from students to teachers and trainers to evaluate the teaching work.

Flexibility in learning

Gives the student the option to decide about the way of learning. Flexibility is a crucial item in self-paced learning.

---

[28] http://www.enqa.eu/

Flipped Classroom

The flipped classroom is a pedagogical model in which the typical lecture and homework elements of a course are reversed.

Formal education

Formal education (from its origin) is classroom based and provided by a trainer or teacher. The students' group does not change and the students are taught by the same teachers.

Formative Evaluation

Formative evaluation is a type of usability evaluation that helps to 'form' the design for a product or service. Formative evaluations involve evaluating a product or service during development, often iteratively, with the goal of detecting and eliminating usability problems.

Formative assessment

To determine the strengths and weakness of student's work assessments are undertaken. They aim to improve the students' learning or their success.

Forum

A forum means a web-based message board. Members of the forum can post messages and others may answer.

In Blended Learning a forum is a tool for interactive cooperation of students.

Independent learning Material

Material that is designed for learners to study with minimal or no assistance by teachers (self-study material)

Informal education

Informal education happens outside the classroom, in after-school programs, community-based organisations, museums, libraries, or at home.

Interactivity

Interactivity can be defined as the "dialogue" between learners and eLearning tools through which learners become engaged and involved in the eLearning process. It is a key element in the eLearning or distance learning design process. Besides that, interactivity can be used to describe the interactions between learners, especially in the distance learning.

Learning design

It describes the process of planning, structuring and sequencing learning activities (this definition is valid for onsite teaching as well as for distance teaching).

Learning management system (LMS)

An LMS is a software application for the administration, documentation, tracking, reporting and delivery of learning or training.

Learning outcomes

Descriptions or statements indicating what targets a learner should have achieved at the end of a given course or learning program.

Competence oriented learning outcomes are described through the three parts knowledge, skills and attitudes and define the competence that a learner should have achieved at the end of learning.

Learning platform

A learning platform is described as a system which focuses on the delivery of the content and the tools needed for distance learning. Sometimes the term Virtual Learning Environment (VLE) is used.

Likert Scale

A response range for a type of survey question in which a person is asked to agree or disagree with a statement. The scale typically runs from 1 ("strongly disagree") to 5 or 7 ("strongly agree") or videvers. With a Likert scale, neither the numerical scores nor the intervals between score values have any intrinsic meaning.

Moderation or moderation

This term means the facilitating of discussions either in onsite teaching situations or in the distance learning. Moderating should keep students engaged, keep the thread and ensure acceptable behavior (especial in online forums).

Module

This is a separate and coherent block of learning.

Open Educational Ressources

Materials offered freely for use by teachers and learners.

Peer assessment

Assessment or review of student's work carried out by other students. Sometimes it is called collegial feedback.

Quality assurance

The maintenance of a desired level of quality for a product or a service is called quality assurance. It means a strict definition, how quality can be checked and who is responsible for it. Do not mess quality assurance with quality control.

Quality control

It means the evaluation of the quality of a product or service to indicate needed corrective activities or amendment processes to meet the desired quality.

Social constructivism

Social constructivism is a variety of cognitive constructivism that emphasises the collaborative nature of much learning.

Storyboard

A technique for illustrating an interaction between a person and a product (or multiple people and multiple products) in narrative format, which includes a series of drawings, sketches, or pictures and sometimes even words that tell a story.

Summative assessment

Assessments leading to the attribution of a grade or a mark to the student. Summative assessments often are executed at the end of the teaching.

Teacher

Teachers usually teach in schools or other organisations involved in formal education.

The term - in origin from Latin - means a kind of official sanction to something or somewhat.

In Blended Learning the author promotes the term to validate the learning in a course from the learner´s view. The learner estimates how much the learning was valid (in the sense of "was it worth to attend the course?").

Trainer

Trainers may work as teachers, but are often working in the field on non-formal education, for example at companies.

The difference between teachers and trainers is getting diffuse in the last years especially in distance learning or mixed methods (Hybrid or Blended Learning).

Tutor

A teacher who provides instructions, various advice or counsel to students.

Usability Evaluation

Assessing the usability of a product with the purpose of identifying usability problems and/or obtaining usability measures. The purpose of evaluation can be to improve the usability of the product as part of design/development (formative evaluation), or to assess the extent to which usability objectives have been achieved (summative evaluation).

Validation

Virtual Learning Environment (VLE)

A VLE is a set of systems or tools with controlled access to students to support the students in their distance learning. Typically, a VLE is accessed by the web, but can also be installed locally in a company to supply the staff in learning.

Web 2.0 tools

They describe modern means to create, edit or share user-generated content. In modern teaching, especial in distance learning, these tools offer the easy collaboration in groups.

WiFi

popular wireless networking technology using radio waves to provide high-speed Internet and network communication

Used Abbreviations

AE	Adult education
CMS	Content Management System
ENQA	European Network for Quality Assurance in Higher Education
GINCO	Grundtvig International Network of Course Organizers
HE	Higher Education
ILOS	Intended Learning Outcomes
IT	Information Technology
LAN	Local area network
LCMS	Learning Content Management System
LMS	Learning Management System
PC	Personal computer
QM	Quality Matters, Inc.
VET	Vocational Education and Training
VLE	Virtual Learning Environment
Wi-Fi	Wireless Internet for Frequent Interface